Transcendence
and
Fulfillment

Transcendence and Fulfillment

*A Critique of Paul's
Seven Pillars of Wisdom and
Their Enduring Relevance*

Benjamin W. Farley

WIPF & STOCK · Eugene, Oregon

TRANSCENDENCE AND FULFILLMENT
A Critique of Paul's Seven Pillars of Wisdom and Their Enduring Relevance

Copyright © 2016 Benjamin W. Farley. All rights reserved. Except for brief quotations in critical publications or reviews, no part of this book may be reproduced in any manner without prior written permission from the publisher. Write: Permissions, Wipf and Stock Publishers, 199 W. 8th Ave., Suite 3, Eugene, OR 97401.

Wipf & Stock
An Imprint of Wipf and Stock Publishers
199 W. 8th Ave., Suite 3
Eugene, OR 97401

www.wipfandstock.com

PAPERBACK ISBN: 978-1-4982-9977-0
HARDCOVER ISBN: 978-1-4982-9979-4
EBOOK ISBN: 978-1-4982-9978-7

Manufactured in the U.S.A.

Unless otherwise noted, all Scripture references are from The New Oxford Annotated Bible with the Apocrypha, edited by Bruce M. Metzger and Roland E. Murphy, New Revised Standard Version, New York: Oxford University Press. Copyright © 1991, Division of Christian Education of the National Council of the Churches of Christ in the United States of America. Used by permission. All rights reserved.

Dedicated to Alice Anne, John and Bryan,
and Luther H. Richenbaker III

Contents

Acknowledgments | ix

1. Paul's Seven Pillars of Wisdom | 1
2. Pillar One—God and the Self: Transcendence | 7
3. Paul of Tarsus and His Knowledge of Jesus | 24
4. Pillar Two—The Consolation of Mysticism | 39
5. Spiritual Consciousness: Its Depths and Dimensions | 51
6. Pillar Three—The Righteousness of God | 66
7. Pillar Four—Apollonian Restraint in a Dionysian Age | 79
8. Pillar Five—Toward Universals That Transform Life | 90
9. Pillar Six—The Delay of the Angels | 103
10. Pillar Seven—Human Fate: Fulfillment and Destiny | 115
11. Fragments, Postulates, and Recurring Questions | 128

Bibliography | 137

Acknowledgments

There are many scholars and friends to whom I am indebted and whose support and ideas have inspired this volume. Above all, I am indebted to Professors Donald G. Miller and Balmer Kelly of Union Theological Seminary in Richmond, Virginia, whose courses in the New Testament first whetted my interest in the historical Jesus and the Apostle Paul. I can never forget them or their interest and scholarship in pursuit of the truth. I am equally indebted to Alice Anne, my wife, for her encouragement and patience during the research and writing of this manuscript. I also wish to thank the staff of the Lutheran Southern Theological Seminary in Columbia, South Carolina, for obtaining resources in a prompt and efficient manner whenever I requested them. My gratitude goes as well to the Reverend Luther Rickenbaker III of Spartanburg, South Carolina, for his theological depth, eloquent style, and friendly support. The same is true of Drs. Ben Sloan, Ellen and Eric Skidmore, and Michael Bragan—faithful friends and colleagues across the years. My equal gratitude and appreciation goes to Professor Amy Willis of Lynchburg College for her constructive critique and suggestions concerning *In the Twilight with God*, which have guided me in the writing of this volume. Finally, I wish to thank Libby Case of Columbia, my friend and editorial assistant, whose keen eye and insistence on excellence have contributed immensely to the project. I would also be remiss not to mention the scores of former students who respectfully endured my lectures on the Old and New Testaments, philosophy, and world religions. As each chapter was written, it was impossible not to think of them.

1. Paul's Seven Pillars of Wisdom

Why seven, one might ask? And why call them "pillars of wisdom" when Paul considered what his era deemed "wise" to be "foolishness" in the sight of God? Was not the wisdom he was offering totally different, indeed a "scandal" in the mind of his time?

As for the number seven, the answer is simple, if not disarming, and, in heart, twofold. The first is by way of inspiration from Prov 9:1, 3, 5–6:

> Wisdom has built her house, she has hewn her seven pillars...
>
> She has sent out her servant-girls, she calls from the highest places...
>
> Come, eat of my bread and drink of the wine I have mixed.
>
> Lay aside immaturity, and live, and walk in the way of insight.

Metaphorically, the above lines provide an intriguing glimpse into the soul of Paul. Both his world and thoughts, his mystical bent and directives, were a "mixture" of "bread and wine," of cross and resurrection, resulting in a search for "maturity" and "insight" with the power to transform life. How much was Hebraic and interpolated from the variant perceptions of the kingdom of God, as either (1) foretold by the prophets, or (2) later inspired by the apocalyptic writings of the Hasmonean period, is still debatable. A similar question prevails concerning the extent to which his views were influenced by his Asian-Cilician background. Though current Pauline scholarship rejects the latter, internal evidence suggests otherwise. In truth, Paul's Hebraic element dominates. Nonetheless, Paul's focus on the death and rising again of the *God-Man*, Jesus, along with his mystical experiences and the empowerment they gave him, are characteristic features of the Hellenistic period. They form the silent background in which his appeal took root, thus making Paul's interpretation of Christianity vital ever since his time.[1]

The second reason for seven pillars is more contemporary. Has the time not come for establishing a method of reassessing Paul's message for an era long past his own, especially at a time when his presuppositions are foreign to the modern mind? Can one still find sufficient insight in his message—in his pillars of wisdom—to build one's house of existence upon it? Even more demanding, can one separate Paul's *personal* understanding of Christ Jesus—his link to the Eternal—from Jesus himself, and still have relevant pillars? Can there be a bonding of time and eternity that so unites the Universal and the particular as to preserve the integrity of the Eternal while fulfilling the longing of the finite, yet that still retains the value of Jesus' historical life? Paul achieved such a synthesis for himself and proclaimed it across Asia Minor and as far west as Rome. For centuries after him, Paul's message spoke to kings and kingdoms alike, achieving perhaps its greatest influence during the Reformation. But times have changed since then, though not the human plight. The Enlightenment provided other perspectives, along with the West's discovery of the ascetic and philosophical views of Oriental religions. The latter offer enlightening perspectives on the phenomenon of transcendence and how it plays out in human life. Nonetheless, Paul's pillars of wisdom still speak to the hearts of countless Christian communities, whether Catholic or Protestant, and even secular perspectives, if one takes a larger view.

One might ask, what are the seven pillars?

---

1. Furnish, *Moral Teaching*, 15.

1. Paul's Seven Pillars of Wisdom

1. God and the Self: Transcendence

Paul's first pillar is built upon the conviction that human beings live by more than a sense of quiet desperation, that life has always beckoned one toward something higher, however difficult it may be to discover or access. It is embedded in every moment of conscious self-searching. It dominates every facet of Paul's thought and comes to fruition in the realization that the highest form of transcendence one can attain is *living unto God in faith through Christ*. For Paul, Christ *is* the focus, lest something less than Christ define transcendence and dilute one's experience of wholeness and joy. It is his way of acknowledging the essence of Proverbs' seven pillars of wisdom, that "the fear of the LORD is the beginning of wisdom, and the knowledge of the Holy One insight" (Prov 9:10)—the sum of the seven pillars.

2. The Consolation of Mysticism

Inseparable from transcendence is Paul's appreciation of the ineffable, of the indefinable mystery of God that enriches life and sets imaginations free to live by the highest nuances that address the human plight. Again, for Paul, that possibility occurs only through Christ; nevertheless, in our contemporary arena, it can happen elsewhere whenever one's heart is open to the mystery of the Eternal as one's companion and not as one's avenger or retaliator. The danger of the latter, however, raises the possibility of the loss of "God's personality" as well as the "personality of the searcher," especially if one becomes absorbed in the Ineffable Cloud of Unknowing. For that reason, philosophy has rightly questioned whether one's contact with the Transcendent is with "reality," or merely an epiphenomenal experience of one's loneliest loneliness. Theology presses the question one step further. If the Transcendent has not, nor cannot, initiate the contact, nor can "interact in history," then humankind's experiences of the Transcendent are purely "mental ascents" of one's own, thus communicating nothing about God, let alone resulting in a "unitive" experience. This "bias" on the part of theology, however, has to be countered on behalf of human experience in general. Any form of "revelation" as such is always a form of transcendence, and its "proof" or "disproof" of a reality beyond the self is a matter of faith and interpretation. The sheer experience of transcendence is often its own reward.

3. The Righteousness of God

For Paul and modern psychology, few orders of the spirit are equal to the healing power of grace. It was present all along in Judaism's experience of God's *hesed* love and redeeming *zedek*, but it took Jesus' death to awaken Paul's eyes to the greatest event of his time. For Paul, the righteousness of God—embedded in the story of Abraham and available now to all through faith in Christ—is the answer to what alone redeems life and gives it meaning. It alone is what makes the kingdom of God a reality now, though its consummation is yet to come.

The question today, however, remains different for us. Simply stated: Is Paul's approach valid for the "universality of humankind"? Can the effectiveness of forgiveness endure, shorn from its rootage in the *mystery of God's personality*, or in the power of the living *God's unique redemptive event in Christ*, without reducing it to a mere ideal or a powerful psychological phenomenon? And if the latter occurs, then what of the remarkable life of him who inspired it: Jesus of Nazareth? Was his cross a tragic accident of history, or a genuine conduit of God's eternal grace? In the end, only faith can answer that question.

4. Apollonian Restraint in a Dionysian Age

The fourth pillar is founded on the understanding that a life without restraint loses its liberty, its potential for full growth and for self-fulfillment. Paul's was an age that wavered between Gnosticism, a vaunted wisdom for the few and elite, and antinomian libertinism, which knew no bounds of indulgence—an age not

1. Paul's Seven Pillars of Wisdom

wholly unlike our own. It was also an age "between the times," between the end of the Old Testament era and the coming of the kingdom of God. To both Gnostics and Antinomians, Paul had to say, "No." On what basis may we say the same?

5. Toward Universals That Transform Life

Paul's fifth pillar of wisdom recognizes that there are definable universal values that are commensurate with self-attainment without mitigating the mystical and transcendent forces that nurture the inward person. Paul knew his era longed for such values, even desiring to live by them, but that it was caught in a web of darkness that blinded its inner vision and paralyzed its will. Beyond the higher values he would come to espouse, Paul would add his immortal three: faith, hope, and love.

6. The Delay of the Angels

No one knows the future, yet to live open to the power of the Transcendent to shape one's future is essential. Granted, today, Pauline eschatology is deemed too remote and esoteric to take seriously; nonetheless, for Paul it was an integral aspect of wisdom. Does it still illuminate existence for our postmodern world?

7. Human Fate: Fulfillment and Destiny

Paul's seventh pillar rests on the understanding that human fate, or one's destiny, does not have to end in despair. For Paul, thanks to Christ, individuals may now grasp their destiny with vigor and courage, making their lives a tabernacle for good. To that extent, each individual is responsible for what he or she believes, does, or becomes, thus underscoring both the reality of the phenomenon of transcendence and its recognition as essential to human fulfillment.

In truth, the seven pillars are interrelated and interwoven throughout Paul's letters. Though the following study attempts to single each out for discussion, the shadows and nuances of the others are always present.

With the above in mind, we proceed to a critique of Paul's theology and its enduring value.

2. Pillar One:
God and the Self—Transcendence

It was Augustine who first declared that he wished only "to know God and the Soul," but never at the expense of imagining himself as anything other than a restless heart longing to find peace in God.[1] Time and again, his commentaries and essays speak of the human condition that ever humbles him before God. This is especially portrayed in Augustine's later soliloquies and throughout his masterpiece: *Confessions*. Nonetheless, in some of Augustine's earlier writings, his piety took the form of what Schweitzer would call "an in-God mysticism," which was different from Paul's, as Augustine truly wanted to ascend the neoplatonic ladder of intellectual ascent (so popular in his day) and thereby become enveloped "in-God."

Paul's soul equally longed to know the truth about God and himself, about his people's ancient aspirations, and his religion's capacity to fulfill his soul. With the rise in the hope of the coming kingdom of God, Paul wanted to be part of its centuries-awaited movement, to be part of its action, and to be *as blessed* by the eternal glory of God as a *mortal may*. Paul writes that he experienced intense moments of mystical unity with the Ineffable, too deep for words, that opened his life to the Eternal. Nonetheless, Paul's transcendent experiences were never quite as ecstatically sustained as Augustine's intellectual ascents as reported in his *Confessions*; rather, Paul's were mediated—though not always—through the living Christ. It is evident, however, that even in those ascents not mediated by Christ, Paul nonetheless experienced moments

---

1. Augustine, *Confessions*, 150–51, 192–93.

of indisputable ecstatic union with "God," if not a sense of being "assimilated" into God's presence. I say "assimilated" because in Christ Paul found a new portal to life—a gateway to God that filled him with a clarity he had never experienced before and that freed him from the binding restrictions of his rabbinical Judaism.

As Karen Armstrong has observed of the time, "no vast ontological gulf separated the human from the divine."[2] Longing for such unification was relevant to the age. That this longing influenced Paul is undeniable. No passage makes this clearer than the following: "I have been crucified with Christ; and *it is no longer I who live*, but it is *Christ who lives in me*. And *the life I now live in the flesh I live by faith in the Son of God*, who loved me and gave himself for me" (Gal 2:20).

Whatever Paul's intention, his verse resounds with the import of a metaphysical statement. It is both declarative and noetic. It is declarative because it asserts without ambiguity Paul's desired self-identity; it is noetic because it is rooted in his intellectual self-understanding, which is what "noetic" means. William James considered the latter a principal aspect of mystical experiences, which in this case is certainly applicable to Paul. James defined the noetic as a state "of insight into depths of truth unplumbed by the discursive intellect." Such a state includes "illuminations, revelations, full of significance and importance, all inarticulate though they remain; and as a rule they carry with them a curious sense of authority for aftertime."[3]

In concert with James, Evelyn Underhill's subsequent study of mysticism provided an equally engaging window into the soul of "spiritual consciousness." Her definition of mysticism also illuminates Paul's. Underhill writes: "Broadly speaking, I understand it [mysticism] to be the expression of the innate tendency of the human spirit towards complete harmony with the transcendental order."[4] As Underhill goes on to state: "This tendency . . . gradually

---

2. Armstrong, *St.Paul*, 58.
3. James, *Varieties*, 300.
4. Underhill, *Mysticism*, xiv.

2. Pillar One: God and the Self—Transcendence

captures the whole field of consciousness" . . . and attains its highest end "in the experience called 'mystical union.'"[5]

Not long after both James' and Underhill's work, Albert Schweitzer offered a similar definition, but he made a distinction in arguing that Paul's *mysticism* (as Schweitzer preferred to address Paul's response to the *Transcendent*) was never an "in-God mysticism" but was instead an "in-Christ mysticism." The former would have been unthinkable to Paul in Schweitzer's mind, as Paul's avowed monotheism could never have embraced the idea of absolute oneness with God. God is God; human beings are not, pure and simple.[6] In spite of this point, however, we find in 1 Corinthians Paul's allusions to a number of mystical experiences that contradict Schweitzer's position, opening Paul to "depths of truth unplumbed by the discursive intellect." Schweitzer would go on to distinguish between what he called "primitive mysticism" and "intellectual mysticism." Primitive mysticism seeks to unite itself with the divine through rituals and ceremonies, whereas intellectual mysticism is "a common possession of humanity." Schweitzer defined the latter as occurring "whenever thought makes the ultimate effort to conceive the relation of the personality to the universal."[7] He concluded that Paul's mysticism was a mixture of the two. Schweitzer further argued that Paul's in-Christ union with God—also available to others—was rooted in Paul's eschatological views and as such intended primarily for the elect.

All three studies shed immense light concerning Paul's life and thought. In his Galatians statement, Paul's proclaimed union with Christ reveals the depth of his noetic experiences, thus becoming the existential nucleus of his consciousness and being. In doing so, Paul set himself on a path that Schleiermacher would express philosophically in his principle concerning the feeling of absolute dependence of the finite upon the infinite. For Schleiermacher, the historical Jesus personified this feeling to perfection, thus making Christ's God-consciousness a gateway to human salvation. For

5. Ibid.
6. Schweitzer, *Mysticism of Paul*, 3–5.
7. Ibid.

Paul, however, it is more than Christ's "God-consciousness" that opens the door to a new life indwelled by God's Spirit; rather, it is Christ's death and resurrection, embracing all humanity—Schweitzer's limitation notwithstanding—that Paul took to be actual events of God's mighty acts of history. For Paul and for theology in general, the latter (that God actually enters history) is what underwrites all faith and, without which, faith would be delusional, or merely an act of human hope and aspiration.

We cannot underestimate Paul's Gal 2:20 passage, because it encapsulates the heart of Pauline theology concerning that alone which fulfills human existence: *the realization that Christ is one's truest link with the Eternal.* One might call it Paul's normative principle, a supposition on which all else is based, especially his ethics. This is true, though his views are laden with presuppositions that were inseparable from his era's cosmological perspective. In addition, Paul incorporated other significant principles he derived principally from a minimum of four sources: (1) his knowledge of the Jesus movement, (2) his understanding of the Messiah as envisioned in the Septuagint and late Jewish apocalyptic writings, (3) his dissatisfaction with rabbinical casuistry, and (4) his fifteen years of concentrated reflection prior to and including the time he first met with Peter, James, and John, or attended the so-called Jerusalem Conference of Acts 12:25.

Let us begin with Paul's presuppositions. All of them were part of the age into which he was born. The first is his acceptance of a realm of transcendence that is superior to any created dominion of time, matter, or space. Both Judaism and Christianity still hold to this cosmological view. Its corollary enjoined what the New Testament scholar John Dominic Crossan has labeled *sarcophobia*, or a fear of the flesh, if not a wary disdain of the physical realm.[8]

This presupposition was not Paul's alone. It predates the apostle, if not Plato, whose mentor Socrates enshrined it in Plato's doctrine of the two realms of what can be known: the one permanent, unbegotten, perfect, and eternal, versus its counterpart in the impermanent, begotten, imperfect, and passing. The one

---

8. Crossan, *Birth of Christianity*, xxiii.

2. Pillar One: God and the Self—Transcendence

represents true Being, the other becoming. The one has ever been, the other is purely derivative. Hinduism knows of the same presupposition under the names of Brahman and Maya, or Purusia and Prakriti, though not identical with Plato's realm of ideas.

As a child of his time, Paul was influenced by this deeply embedded cultural view. In truth, he never thought to challenge it, nor did few others, save the Sophists. It was a factor of everyone's Weltanschauung. Even Jesus shared it. Said Jesus, "God is Spirit and those who worship God must worship him in spirit and in truth" (John 4:24). For Paul and Jesus, there is no way to escape the phenomenon of transcendence—that spiritual dimension that puts one's self-understanding in question, resulting in either a heightened or disturbing consciousness of one's relationship with God. Speaking of this condition of humankind in general, Paul writes: "For what can be known about God is plain to them. Ever since the creation of the world his eternal power and divine nature, invisible though they are, have been understood and seen through the things he has made" (Rom 1:20).

That is primal transcendence in its most latent form, waiting only to be seized and appropriated as the guiding light of one's soul. Years before Paul, Plato wrestled with a similar, though purely intellectual, form of transcendence, as his mind ascended "upward" toward the highest concepts reason can conceive. Plato's legacy dominated the Greco-Asian world, even among those who had never heard of him or read a single word of his works.

At first glance, there is nothing wrong with this view. Of course, the unbegotten precedes all derivative existence. It represents the idea of the Transcendent in its fullest cosmological and ontological essence. That Being should be prior to Non-being is logical, otherwise Non-being is self-contradictory. If Non-being existed before Being, then it would have the metaphysical value of Being. For this reason, the philosophical as well as the scientific conundrum of how anything came from nothing begs the question that countless efforts have sought to resolve. In our modern era, Hume came as close as anyone to resolving it in his maxim "like effects require like causes," or at a minimum, "equal causes." Thus

Being precedes what is begotten, rendering the idea of Non-being to the putative opposite of Being. It is when one identifies one's finite and begotten beingness with Being itself that metaphysical boundaries are crossed, which in its most extreme form results in the philosophical position known as monism—that all things are one and the self is nothing more than an extension of the One.

Paul's struggles with his weaknesses and inner doubts prevented him from falling into such a pitfall, yet he clearly identified his existential being with Christ's risen life, along with the abolishment of his old self; nonetheless, it is this proclivity that requires attention if we are to appropriate the value of transcendence in our own lives. The abolishment of the old self might be true from a "spiritual" viewpoint, but it establishes a discontinuity of the present self with its unique former self in a way that belies the human condition and the integrity of one's genuine individuality or personality.

That Paul could not have known this should be recognized, as no one wishes to judge Paul from an anachronistic position. Judging Paul on this basis clearly commits the fallacy known as *nunc pro tunc* ("now for then"), a bias that holds the past responsible for a range of knowledge inaccessible or unknowable at the time. Yet, if our contemporary era is to draw insight from Paul's views, adapting them to our perspective is essential. Whatever the self is, it is both a physiological and psychological continuation of its past development; it is a self-conscious moment of its flowing concurrent experiences, all held in anticipation of what is next. The spiritual abolishment of one's former self does not erode the existential "essence" of one's present self with its connectivity to its past or to its uncertain future. One can be wary of the "old self's" power to thwart one's present and future hope, but one is still the same person. Judaism rejected the continuity of the self with God, though it well understood the reality of the Transcendent and the wholeness it offered. "Whither shall I go from thy presence or flee from thy Spirit?" (Ps 139:7, KJV).

Paul, as a child of his age, embodied the "Platonic ideal" of transcendence in its most integrative form, resulting in a freedom

2. Pillar One: God and the Self—Transcendence

and deliverance he had never imagined possible. The Platonic understanding of transcendence fit in beautifully with Paul's own Hebraic heritage of one, sole, eternal God, from whom alone all else is derived. Paul might never have read a single dialogue of Plato's works, nor does he mention the luminary by name, but the Platonic worldview of transcendence, with its high defining universals, was a tacit presupposition of the Greco-Asian era. We cannot know if it was a factor in Paul's "formal" education, since his commitment to his Hebraic tradition prevails. However, if Paul knew anything of Philo of Alexandria, then the synthesis of Hebraic thought with Plato's ideas was already rooted in his subconsciousness. As for Paul's knowledge of Stoicism, it is a well-recognized aspect of Paul's intellectual heritage.[9]

Paul's existential and ontological identification of his inner self with the Transcendent (become historical in Christ) leads to a second presupposition of the time: that the created order of life's cycles, its struggles and opportunities, its brevity and limits—indeed the whole physical realm—pales in comparison to the attainment of life's highest good. Like Orpheus' "prison house of the soul," the body itself is but an "earthly tent," destined to pass away (1 Cor 5:1). Plato's *Apology*, Aristotle's *Nicomachean Ethics*, and Epicurus' views all entertained the same premise. As in the case of transcendence, such a view, when carried to the extreme, created yet another disconnect with Paul's Jewish heritage by introducing into Christianity a Greco-Asian motif foreign to its Hebraic past. Consider the following.

In the Old Testament the (*hesed*) love of God, along with God's zeal for justice and righteousness (*zedek*), never endorses a diminution of the physical realm's worth. Rather, it assigns paramount importance to the present, to the now, not solely to a transcendent realm or some distant time to come in the future. Life's wealth of riches is to be enjoyed and shared, not renounced or avoided. We are creatures of flesh and spirit, not simply spirit. Nor is the life of created matter to be defined in demeaning terms, such as Paul does in his letters. Unbegotten, eternal, imperishable, and perfect

9. Murphy-O'Connor, *Paul: His Story*, 5–6.

Being belongs to God. The begotten, mortal, perishable, and finite qualities of beingness belong to humankind. Understanding this biblical injunction preserves the idea of God as holy, eternal, and ineffable; yet it supports the conviction that human life is nonetheless "a little lower than God's" (Ps 8), with a divinely-endowed worth all its own. Paul's presupposition regarding the low estate of "the flesh" compromises its divine dignity, which he considered lost, thereby undermining the true gifts of humankind's potential in the present.

Paul was comfortably at home in believing that only minds, wills, and hearts transformed by a transcendent love of God in Christ can experience life's highest fulfillment, free of the distractions of the physical realm and its fall into sin. His view still carries an incontestable truth. From Socrates to the present, transcendence in its noblest form has inspired the world. But that is not the question. The problem is exacerbated by the fact that in Paul's mind, the end time was coming. The physical world was passing away and was therefore less deserving of full commitment or value. Christ would soon return, though when, no one knew. Nevertheless, Paul's belief in the end time, with all the chaos that would be predicted to ensue, set Christianity on a course that led, by the end of the second century CE, to a retreat from the worthiness of the vocational calls of the created order. In Schweitzer's mind, the Parousia's delay actually exacerbated the transformation from Paul's "in-Christ mysticism" to an "in-God mysticism," significantly altering, if not corrupting, Paul's original dynamic. For Schweitzer, John's Gospel clearly reflects this change, as well do the letters of Ignatius. It would take the Reformation to reverse this course in its own trans-valuation of transcendence.

A third unexamined presupposition revolves around the satanic forces and demonic dimensions that the ancient world feared were endemic to human existence. Assuming them to be real (i.e., genuine) metaphysical entities that enjoy conscious awareness and will, Pauline theology casts the human struggle as one pitted not only against the temptations of the flesh, but also against the very powers of darkness that thwart human wholeness and fulfillment.

2. Pillar One: God and the Self—Transcendence

In Christ's crucifixion and resurrection, these forces have been dealt a deathblow; nonetheless, they are operative in the world and must be confronted as well as denied authority in one's life. Paul is fully cognizant of their power and knows that it is only at the end time, with its final judgment, that they will be condemned and ultimately destroyed. Nevertheless, they are present now and must be contested.

Not surprisingly, however, Paul tamps down their influence wherever he can, confident of their final end. He mentions them less often than do the gospels. Paul refers to "Satan" only eight times in his authentic writings, and he refers to "demons" twice, along with "the powers of this age" or "elemental spirits" twice. Perhaps the most notable of his references is the passage in Rom 8:38. It captures the Hellenistic period's fear of the unknown and its spirits, as well as its fallen angels and their disastrous impact on humankind. "For I am convinced that neither death, nor life, nor angels, nor rulers, nor things present, nor things to come, nor powers, nor height, nor depth, nor anything else in all creation will be able to separate us from the love of God in Christ Jesus our Lord" (Rom 3:38–39).

Note that his list of perils concentrates on both the physical realm as well as the celestial. Known today as the gospels' "three-storied universe," with heaven above, earth in the center, and hell and its demons below, this was the spiritual equivalent of the Ptolemaic sevenfold view of the universe, whose coming perspective was less than a century away. Paul's list encompasses it all. His inventory includes life and death, political rulers as well as evil spirits, the present as well as the future, the intermediate powers of the upper and lower worlds that operate between God and Hades, Earth's anxieties and uncertainties, and the burdensome weight of a fallen creation. Like the rebellious rulers of Ps 2 who have set their faces against God and his anointed, all are arraigned against any human spirit that would strive to live free of impediments. Although Paul recognizes numerous opportunities for human engagement within God's created realm (Rom 12:1–21), Paul nonetheless views the created order as captive to an array of evil powers committed to assaulting human life and its full attainment. Thus, he appeals to God's underpinning of supra-transcendence to battle life's intervening foes.

In this regard, we are humbled to remember the dramatic currents that were associated in Paul's era with the coming of the Messiah and the esoteric fantasies it created. For example, the book of Enoch traces the story of Enoch's ascension into heaven, where Enoch learns of the so-called "Watchers of Heaven" and their ruinous impact (*1 Enoch* 14–16). This is instrumental in understanding something of Paul's interior views concerning the rulers and powers of this world:

> Go speak to the Watchers of Heaven: . . . Why did you leave lofty, holy Heaven to sleep with women, to defile yourselves with the daughters of men and take them as your wives, and like the children of the earth to beget sons, in your case giants? . . . But you were spiritual and immortal for all generations of the world. So I gave you no wives, for Heaven is your proper dwelling place. And now the giants, offspring of spirit and flesh, will be called spirits on the earth, and earth shall be their dwelling . . . The giants afflict, oppress, destroy, attack over the earth . . . Their spirits will rise up against men and women because they proceed from them.[10]

Of such is the human predicament for Paul, haunted on earth by these fallen powers, whose purpose now is to torment, harass, and mislead humankind.

It is interesting to note, however, that Paul's Jewish heritage rejected this view. From its earliest Mosaic roots, not even the Shema summoned its adherents to such a suspicious or combative view of God's created order. "Hear, O Israel: the LORD is our God, the LORD alone. You shall love the LORD your God with all your heart, and with all your soul, and with all your might. Keep these words . . . in your heart. Recite them to your children . . . talk about them when you are at home and when you are away, when you lie down and when you rise" (Deut 6:4–7).

---

10. Barnstone, *Other Bible*, 487.

2. Pillar One: God and the Self—Transcendence

This remarkable insight has to do with life *now*, carried out through one's center of essential vitality (the heart), to be shared with one's children in one's home, cutting across one's occupation and travels, and guarding and guiding one's activities by day or by night. It is meant to buoy the soul through life's quotidian hardships and inescapable encounters with reality, not to be a mantra for escape from the "slings and arrows of outrageous fortune."[11] It is this sphere in which God becomes real or not. It is here, in God's earthly realm, with all its tribulations, ironies, disappointments, and "demons," that God summons the faithful to believe in God, to persevere, and to build God's kingdom on earth. One could argue that even Jesus' "Lord's Prayer" echoes the Shema in a quieter, though equally relevant, form, and yet that it shares with Paul the fear of "being led into temptation" by either God's divine will or, more horrifyingly, by the powers of the fallen apocalyptic ruling angels.

Paul's notion of creation's groaning for its own deliverance (Rom 8:22) is part of his *sarcophobia*, or fear of the physical realm. In Paul's view, it has lost its divinely blessed status and has become "subjected to futility" and the "bondage to decay" (Rom 8:20–21). It has slipped into the darkness of fallen powers. The biblical fall, however, clearly contests this assessment. In the Genesis story, the fall pertains to human beings, not to nature. It is human beings whose distaff must bear their children in pain, whose fields challenge humankind with briars and stone and fertile soil that fallen humanity must now plow in sweat. Why? Because of human obstinacy, not because the *adamah*, or soil—which God created and from which YHWH fashioned human life—has suddenly lost its virility or become demon-possessed. The fault is purely due to humankind's pride, doubt, and arrogant spirit. Pride and arrogance despoil the human attempt to live transcendentally, because pride and arrogance are foreign to transcendence. The earth itself is good; it remains wholly *tov*. Any harsh qualities associated with it redound to humankind's opportunity to take them in stride while seeking to advance God's kingdom on earth.

11. Shakespeare, *Hamlet*, act 3, scene 1.

Again, to Paul's credit, he acknowledges life's crushing reach. Nonetheless, in his mind, "neither hardship, nor distress, nor persecution, nor famine, nor nakedness, nor peril, nor sword can separate one from the love of God in Christ" (Rom 8:28). Embracing the Transcendent enables one to endure as well as conquer these hardships, whether of opposing spirits or of nature. Unity with Christ makes all this possible, while Christ's intercession with God secures one's deliverance from the incongruities of existence. This is all welcome and heartfelt news; nevertheless, it clearly reveals a focus different from the simpler summons of Jesus' inaugural sermon. "The time [*kairos*] is fulfilled. The kingdom of God is at hand. Repent and believe in the good news" (Mark 1:15). Jesus' proclaimed *kairos* is a time for gratitude and action, for joy and progress, and for personal accountability, however helpful asceticism and religious quiescence are to the human spirit and no matter how distant or near the kingdom of God might be. Human beings are still who they are: existential selves whose past and present consciousness is enfolded into the heart of God even while upholding their unique individuality.

Luther captured this when he rightfully concluded that Christians are *simultaneously sinful and justified*. Their sinfulness is forgiven and their brokenness mended by the wounds of Christ, but they remain uniquely who they are, which leads to the following question: Was Paul too eager for a transformation that would lift one out of this morass? Is that why the ascetic world of Platonic forms—whether he knew of them directly or indirectly—appealed to Paul as applicable to the efficacy of Jesus' cross and resurrection? Is it possible—though Pauline scholarship is swift to reject it—that in his *cultural subconscious*, Paul thought of Christ as the biblical equivalent of a Prometheus or a Dionysus and thus the embodiment of that Universal Spirit or élan that saves humankind, even as Paul found Christ's lordship superior to Augustus', whom the Senate of Rome had designated as the Empire's savior (*soter*) only four decades earlier? One cannot help but ask this question. Paul's Christ comes to us as both *human* and *divine* (Phil 2:6–8), as a descendent of the house of David, yet as one who emptied himself of

2. Pillar One: God and the Self—Transcendence

his divinity in order to become human. He is no longer just Israel's long-awaited Messiah, but also the Savior of the world. Thus Paul's ontological identity becomes inseparable from his spiritual union with the *divine* Christ, who, appearing in a particular human life, redeems and empowers Paul's own life, though he remains captive to *the flesh*. However indebted Paul might have been to later Judaism's apocalyptical understanding of the kingdom of God and its Son of Man, or Ancient One, a *divine-human* Christ makes sense only in a world that had already appropriated this concept and all its possibilities into its myths of dying and rising divine heroes. This is the ingredient that is so often denied by opponents of this position.

Life's powers of darkness, however, did not end with the ascendancy of Christ's triumph of the world. The end time had yet to come. The powers of evil that tempt human minds are not so easily toppled. Today we know them as facets of human choice, mirrored in the limits of human finitude, our DNA, belief systems, and habituation. One thinks of the late medieval period and the fact that Martin Luther's famous hymn of Ps 46 is beset by the fear of the demonic: "For still our ancient foe dost seek to work us woe, his craft and power are great, and armed with cruel hate, on earth is not his equal."

Nor did Calvin's Geneva fare better. Few historians have cut through its darker legacy as powerfully as Paul Kriwaczek in his *Yiddish Civilisation: The Rise and Fall of a Forgotten Nation*. After describing the brutality and backwardness of the age, he writes:

> That is not to say that John Calvin was at heart in any way a man of gentle disposition. He was not. In the first four years of the theocratic totalitarian tyranny he founded in Geneva, he had fifty-eight heretics consigned to the stake and seventy-six exiled: in one single year he had forty-three women burned as witches; during a three-month outbreak of plague he executed thirty-four unfortunates for "sowing the pest." In 1553 he unforgivably sent to the pyre the brilliant Michael Servetus . . . though it is said

that Calvin would have preferred a less brutal form of execution.[12]

Not to mention the hanging of witches in Salem during the reign of the Puritans in New England.

Luther, Calvin, and the founders of the Plymouth Colony were avid followers of Paul's theology. Their love of Christ need not be doubted, nor need a more "enlightened" age condemn their Christian views. The point is that we humans are flesh and spirit, *ru'ah* and *adamah*, *pneuma* and *sarx*. Our existential complexity is inseparable from our past, our struggles of the present, and our anticipations of the future. It is very much one's existential self that motivates one to embody the spirit of Jesus' love, though confined in an "earthen vessel," as Paul himself was forced to acknowledge in his moments of stark lucidity and self-reflection (2 Cor 4:7).

Transcendence has its healing balm with power to mend all ailing hearts. To deny this would betray the very power and comfort, direction and enlightenment that all religions seek. It would also neutralize the human heart's own experience of the reality of the nearness of God that speaks to one's deepest self. More than anything, this awareness captures the essence of Paul's love of Christ, whose death and resurrection transformed his sense of God's nearness into a *reality* and not just a *hope* or facet of Hellenistic idealism. In truth, Paul rightfully gave the world this vision of historical attainment in spite of the Weltanschauung that shaped his understanding of the phenomenon of transcendence. Celebrating Paul's Christ Jesus and Paul himself as *historical exemplars* of the appropriation of the highest and holiest reality the mind can conceive is relevant to all time.

By way of critique, however, Günter Bornkamm took exception with much of the above. In his book entitled *Paul*, Bornkamm rejected any attempts to assess Paul's Christ Jesus as a "concept of God" or the "idea of God" imposed upon the figure of Jesus.[13] We have noted that Albert Schweitzer rejected the same temptation,

---

12. Kriwaczek, *Yiddish*, 178.
13. Bornkamm, *Paul*, 237.

2. Pillar One: God and the Self—Transcendence

observing that any direct appropriation of the divine was foreign to Paul's thought and could only be achieved through a Mediator. Bornkamm's work, however, was generated in the late 1960s as a culmination of the quest for the historical Jesus in Bornkamm's day. Since Bornkamm's period, the latest quest of the historical Jesus—as represented in the works of the Jesus Society and the scholars of the Five Gospels, the discovery of the Nag Hammadi Library as well as the Qumran scrolls, and in Crossan's probing analyses of Jesus as sage and revolutionary—has brought new "evidence" to light in the role that gnostic, Platonic, and Roman imperialism played in shaping Christianity's first-century views. Factors other than eschatology, on which Schweitzer launched his Pauline masterpiece, were at play. To these factors we must return, but there are philosophical considerations of Paul's identity with Christ that deserve review and can enrich our personal search for fulfillment.

It is Søren Kierkegaard who, in modern times, has forced theologians to ponder the problems and possibilities raised by any "self's" relationship with the divine. These problems and possibilities have to do with Kierkegaard's analysis of the self's relationship with itself and of that self's relationship, in turn, to God. In both Kierkegaard's *Fear and Trembling* and *The Sickness Unto Death*, he restates the problem in numerous ways. Both essays represent the Dane's reflections on God's call to Abraham to offer his son Isaac as a sacrifice to God. It involves a philosophical dalliance, even a teleological suspension of the ethical, between the "universal and the particular, the eternal and the individual," as well as "the inward and the outward," to quote his words.[14] It addresses the age-old problem of how the individual can appropriate anything of the Eternal while remaining finite and particular. Does not the Eternal negate the concept that the temporal can appropriate anything of the Eternal—at least in the equivocal sense—or that the particular can appropriate the Universal to any meaningful degree? Rejecting Hegel's theory of the Absolute, which unfolds in history to shape and determine human life, Kierkegaard focused on Abraham's relationship with God to propose an engaging solution.

---

14. Kierkegaard, *Fear*, 146.

In brief, each person's self is in relationship with itself and, as such, is a "synthesis" of the self in its relation with itself. But the self, in relating itself to the self, is also relating itself to that Power which constitutes the whole phenomenon of relation.[15] Kierkegaard defines the self as Spirit and Spirit as self. This relationship forms the synthesis that binds the essential elements of humankind's nature. Writes Kierkegaard, "Man is a synthesis of the infinite and the finite, of the temporal and the eternal, of freedom and necessity."[16] But so regarded, "man is not yet a self." It is only when that self is in relationship with the "Power which constituted the whole relation" that the self can "attain and remain in equilibrium,"[17] for "by relating itself to its own self and by willing to be itself the self is grounded transparently in the Power which posited it."[18]

Would Paul have agreed with Kierkegaard that from a "spiritual" viewpoint, Kierkegaard's position is precisely what he was trying to articulate? That only the extent to which Paul stood in an "absolute" relationship with God, which only God could make possible, could Paul experience his life fulfilled as an "ontological" new creation—as a self in equilibrium with itself? Yet, for Paul, even that was only possible because of the death and resurrection of Christ, who, as the Universal Son of God, took on flesh, thus becoming a particular individual and thereby representing the particular in every human being as well as preparing the self for the status of becoming "higher than the universal." Through one man, Christ, all humans now enjoy the power and the presence of the Personal Transcendent Universal that cleanses and renews their finite existence.

For Kierkegaard and Paul, the efficacy of this relationship, or of humankind's absolute relationship with the Absolute, rests on "faith." Both Paul and Kierkegaard cite the Patriarch Abraham's belief in God's promise as pivotal to their understanding of human

15. Ibid.
16. Ibid.
17. Ibid., 147.
18. Ibid.

2. Pillar One: God and the Self—Transcendence

wholeness. For Paul, the death of the promised Messiah caught everyone off-guard, becoming something of a "scandal," while for Kierkegaard, the Abrahamic drama involved an absurdity, a paradox that only "faith" can fathom. Writes Kierkegaard:

> Faith is precisely this paradox, that the individual as the particular is higher than the universal, is justified over against it, is not subordinate but superior—yet in such a way, be it observed, that it is the particular individual who, after he has been subordinated as the particular to the universal, now through the universal becomes the individual who as the particular is superior to the universal, for the fact that the individual as the particular stands in an absolute relation to the absolute.[19]

Granted, the above captures transcendence in its highest philosophical form; nonetheless, it provides spiritual illumination for the human condition. Whatever one may think of Kierkegaard's "existentialism," his analysis of the self in relation to the Absolute captures Paul's own hunger for a self-fulfillment, which compelled him to proclaim: "it is no longer I who live but it is Christ who lives in me" (Gal 1:20). In this unification of Paul's individuality with Christ's universality, the particular in Paul became greater than the *universal condition that defines human existence*. As Schweitzer, reflecting on Paul's attainment to this end, comments, Paul's "greatest achievement was to grasp, as the thing essential to being a Christian, the experience of union with Christ."[20] And that is precisely what Gal 1:20 celebrates.

Schweitzer would go on to offer that by "simply designating Jesus 'our Lord' Paul raises Him above all the temporally conditioned conceptions in which the mystery of His personality might be grasped." In so doing, Paul set "Him forth as the Spiritual Being, who transcends all human definitions, to whom we have to surrender ourselves in order to experience in Him the true law of our existence and our being."[21]

---

19. Ibid., 66.
20. Schweitzer, *Mysticism of Paul*, 377.
21. Ibid., 379.

3. Paul of Tarsus and His Knowledge of Jesus

Scholars differ widely as to what Paul actually knew about Jesus. Remember, it was a time of anticipation, and it was the yearning for the coming of Israel's long-awaited Messiah that aroused hopes in Paul's time. The Dead Sea Scrolls of Qumran, with their emphasis on the imminence of the coming of both a priestly and a political Messiah, along with the esoteric writings preserved in *Psalm of Solomon* and *1 Enoch* were in the air. The Baptist's appearance, along with Jesus', seemed to set the stage. Indeed, the time was right for the appearance of the king whom the Solomon passage hails as "the son of David . . . the LORD Messiah" (*Pss. Sol.* 17). In that light, it is not surprising that Paul rarely mentions the historical Jesus by name. His concerns are for the Messiah, who has come to initiate the kingdom, who will come again to fulfill it, and who is God's Son, descended from the house of David. It is this person, this reality, this event that absorbs Paul's interest rather than the Jesus of Nazareth, whose story had yet to be written. For Paul, the good news is about "Christ Jesus," or "Jesus Christ our Lord," crucified and raised from the dead, whose meaning must be seized, proclaimed, and expounded.

Paul rarely refers to "Jesus" by name, although in 2 Corinthians he does mention the name of "Jesus" at least five times, but only in reference to his death and resurrection. Otherwise, in something of an inverse proportion, Paul refers to Jesus as the "Christ" no less than two-hundred-and-forty-one times. In contrast, the Gospels mention the name "Christ" only five times: three in John's Gospel and twice in Mark's. For Paul, Christ has already superseded the historical Jesus in terms of the role he plays in enabling followers

3. Paul of Tarsus and His Knowledge of Jesus

to become "new creations" in the kingdom of God. This should give pause to any reader from the start, for it emphasizes *Paul's estimate of Jesus* as the divinely revealed Redeemer sent from God to rescue and liberate all humankind, *rather than focusing on the historical Jesus* and his unique message concerning the in-breaking of God's kingdom. Such is the role of the Universal Christ over the individual in all of his or her individuality. Paul makes it clear: "From now on, therefore, we regard no one from a human point of view; though we once knew Christ from a human point of view, we know him no longer in that way. So if anyone is in Christ, there is a new creation: everything old has passed away; see, everything has become new" (2 Cor 5:16–17).

This is not to say that Paul knew *only* of Jesus' death and resurrection. Undoubtedly he gleaned significant information from a variety of encounters with Jesus' followers. F. F. Bruce argues that Paul was familiar with a number of Jesus' statements, which he possibly acquired while Paul was in Antioch or during his fifteen-day visit in Jerusalem with Peter. In his book *Paul, Apostle of the Heart Set Free*, Bruce references no less than five major subject headings echoing sayings attributed to Jesus. Paul uses these "quotes" to support the authority of his own message. Bruce catalogs these five areas as divorce and marriage, the laborer's just wages, the approval of the eating of Gentile foods, tribute to whom tribute is due, and various forms of the Golden Rule concerning the repayment of evil with good.

In accordance with each subject above, Bruce cites the following verses, first in Paul's letters and then in their gospel form: (1) 1 Cor 7:10, Mark 10:11; (2) 1 Cor 9:14, Luke 10:7; (3) 1 Cor 10:27, Luke 10:8; (4) Rom 13:7, Mark 12:13; and (5) Gal 6:1–2, Rom 12:14, and 12:21, with Matt 18:15, Luke 6:27–28, and Mark 12:28f.[1]

It would behoove us, however, to keep in mind that Paul's knowledge of any of Jesus' sayings circulated in oral form (including what he learned from his visit with Peter), or possibly in some earlier drafts of Q. Paul's letters predate the appearance of the

---

1. Bruce, *Paul*, 105–112.

gospels, even Mark's, which the early church believed was based on Peter's sermons. In fairness to Paul, there is no way he could have known multiple sayings of Jesus'. The movement was in its infancy and, unlike Israel's fascination with Ezra's Torah, which its rabbis had committed to memory in the form of the Tradition of the Elders, Jesus' sayings were still undergoing a sifting-out process regarding authentic words and deeds versus claims and truth. Q would represent just one of these collections, Paul's references to "tradition" (1 Cor 11:23) would make up a second, and the 114 sayings in the *Gospel of Thomas* would represent a third (provided the latter were even circulating).

What makes it difficult to reconstruct what Paul knew of the Jesus movement or of the historical Jesus is due in part to present-day historians' doubts concerning the veracity of Luke's Acts. Nowhere does Luke mention any of Paul's letters, nor does he call into question the significant rift that was widening between the Hellenistic followers of Christ and Jerusalem's more staid Hebraic disciples. Luke knew about the rift, but he chose not to dramatize it. Today's consensus wagers that although Luke knew of the pending break, he smoothed it over since it had faded into history, at least by the point in time from which Luke was writing (somewhere close to 80–90 CE, by contemporary assessment). Thus, it is problematic and subjective to recreate Paul's firsthand knowledge of the Jesus movement, its historical trajectory, events, "miracles," or Jesus' actual words. Contrary to Bruce, Bornkamm focuses more on Paul's role as an interpreter of Christ as Redeemer than as an expounder of Jesus' actual words or message.[2]

Nevertheless, one can reconstruct Paul's tentative biography and something of his bustling itinerary. Summarizing contemporary scholarship on the subject, Stephen Harris pieces together what rudimentary facts the New Testament preserves concerning Paul's life and journeys.[3] He warns that any evidence from Acts must be viewed with caution. For, as we have indicated, the latter warning is a guiding norm for almost all Pauline scholarship

2. Bornkamm, *Paul*, 110, 235–37.
3. Harris, *New Testament*, 305–309.

3. Paul of Tarsus and His Knowledge of Jesus

today. What major information, then, does Paul's principal letters (Galatians, 1-2 Corinthians, 1 Thessalonians, Philippians, Philemon, and Romans) provide?

Harris lists the following: Paul was born of a Hellenistic Jewish family (of Tarsus, according to Acts). The date is uncertain, but it was likely around 13 CE. Concerning Paul's family, the Catholic scholar Jerome Murphy-O'Connor emphasizes what Paul himself states: that he was extremely proud of his Jewish heritage, circumcised as he was on the eighth day, of the people of Israel, of the tribe of Benjamin, as a Hebrew born of Hebrews and, as to the Law, a Pharisee (Phil 3:4-5). Based on Murphy-O'Connor's research, Paul's parents were originally from Galilee and were sold into slavery following Rome's destruction of Sepphoris—a major city in Upper Galilee that rebelled against the Jerusalem government following Herod's death. Taken as booty, they were sold to wealthy clients in Tarsus, where they later received freedom and became Roman citizens. Murphy-O'Connor speculates that Paul's parents were something of elitists, inasmuch as Paul tends to look down on common labor, exhibiting "a snobbish leisured class attitude towards manual labour" and regarding it "slavish" and "demeaning" (1 Cor 9:19; 2 Cor 11:7).[4] O'Connor further speculates that Paul likely attended the "University of Tarsus," where he engaged in a curriculum devoted to rhetoric, language, syntax, and philosophy.

After arriving in Palestine (ostensibly to study under Gamaliel), Paul engaged in harassing members of the early Jesus movement. Passages in both 1 Corinthians and Galatians attest as much. At some point during this period (32-34 CE), Paul experienced a "revelation" involving the risen Jesus (Gal 1:12, 16; 1 Cor 15:9-10) while somewhere in the vicinity of Damascus. Whether Luke's account in Acts 9:1-9 describes it accurately cannot be verified. Paul refers to the experience as a "revelation" (*apokalypsis*) whose impact changed his life, but whether it was a "mystical" or "cognitive" revelation is uncertain, at least in the Galatians passage. In the Corinthians passage, the revelation is described as a mystico-visual phenomenon. Paul calls it an "appearance," capturing the

---

4. Murphy-O'Connor, *Paul: His Story*, 2-4.

"event" using the word *ophthé*, a term from which our words "optical" and "ophthalmology" and others having to do with "sight" or "seeing" are derived. Just as Christ "appeared" (optically or cognitively) to Peter and James, so he "appeared" to Paul. Whether an optical revelation or a spiritual one, it "dawned" on Paul that the crucified Jesus was clearly the Messiah, the One his nation had been awaiting for centuries.

Following this "revelation," Paul traveled to Arabia (likely Petra), then returned to Damascus. Three years later, Paul visited Jerusalem to meet Peter and James, Jesus' brother (Gal 1:18–19). Afterwards, Paul returned to Asia to the region of Syria and Cilicia (his homeland), considering himself Christ's appointed apostle to the Gentiles (Gal 1:22).

It was only after fifteen years had passed that Paul journeyed again to Jerusalem, this time with Titus and Barnabas, to attend the Jerusalem Conference concerning the admission of Gentiles to the church. He then returned to Antioch, where he fell into a dispute with Peter over the latter's scruples about eating with Gentiles, then Paul set off on his second and later his third missionary journeys. Paul returned to Jerusalem one last time before Luke's book of Acts traces the story of his arrest, imprisonment at Caesarea, and eventual voyage to Rome.

Discrepancies between Paul's letters and Luke's Acts deserve acknowledgment, although their importance remains questionable. Nowhere in his letters does Paul mention his birth at Tarsus or allude to Rabbi Gamaliel. Of most importance, however, is Acts' report that Ananias was instrumental in Paul's baptism and Paul's reception of the Holy Spirit, whereas Paul insists that he owed his apostolic commission to *no one but Christ* and does not once refer to his baptism. As for Acts' account that Paul agreed to impose dietary restrictions on Gentiles and to ban the eating of meat offered to idols, Paul's letters make it explicit that he refused to agree to such limitations (see Gal 2:5; 1 Cor 8:10:27; Rom 14:13–15:6). One's conscience is free and, in the spirit of Christ, is one's best guide.

3. Paul of Tarsus and His Knowledge of Jesus

None of this, however, scratches the surface of Paul's grasp of the historical Jesus' true significance: that he was crucified, dead, and buried; that he was raised to life again; and that on the evening of his betrayal, he instituted the Lord's Supper (1 Cor 11:23–26). Note his use of the word "betrayal," suggesting that he knew at least an abbreviated inventory of historical facts associated with Jesus' crucifixion. His mentioning of the institution of the Supper, however, is of essential significance, as the event ties in with Paul's theological interpretation of Christ's basic mission. For Paul, the Supper has to do with Jesus as God's heaven-sent Redeemer, for which the breaking of the loaf and the drinking of the cup symbolize Christ's "body and blood" broken and shed for sin as a sign of God's new covenant with Israel, which is to be celebrated until his return.

Paul claims that he received this tradition *"from the Lord,"* not from others. But if so, in what form? Or was it Paul's own "interpretation" of the "love feast" that followers of Jesus were observing in memory of him before the idea of the breaking of the bread and the drinking of the cup were interpreted as symbolic of Christ's founding the new covenant? One has the feeling that both were involved and that the Corinthians version became favored, inasmuch as Paul was instrumental in "passing it on" and setting it in writing before Mark incorporated it in his Passion Narrative. John knows of no such Supper, only of the Passover Seder and the washing of the disciples' feet. Yet in his interpretation of the Feeding of the Five Thousand, John clearly refers to the "eating of the flesh" and the "drinking of the blood" of Jesus as alone insuring "eternal life." "Very truly I tell you, unless you eat the flesh of the Son of Man and drink his blood, you have no life in you" (John 6:53–54). This is far beyond Paul's interpretation and closer to the Asian rites of the mystery cults, but it remains significant because it forces us to ask: Did Paul "impose" on Jesus' Passover meal *a mystical interpretation of redemption* inspired by the Hellenistic cults of his own homeland, thus shifting the focus of the original eating of the Passover lamb, whose blood was shed to protect the Hebrew people during Israel's deliverance, into a redemption event for all humankind, represented in the symbolic eating of the flesh of a god and the drinking of its blood? Certainly Paul identifies the Lord's Supper with the "body and blood" of Christ, which are not to be consumed lightly by his followers (1 Cor 11:27). If the word "impose," however, is too strong and lacks "textual evidence," Paul's Cilician background nonetheless prompts one to infer that its influence shaped his interpretation of the Supper.

One doubts that the truth can ever be known, but since Paul's tradition of the Lord's Supper was written prior to Mark's, one is tempted to suspect that Paul's version shaped the gospels narratives themselves and their explanations of the event, notwithstanding the nuances of a "pre-tradition" of which Paul was aware. In it, the God-sent Redeemer is "remembered" not only for the inauguration of God's kingdom now and to come, but also as one's conduit to a fulfilled life, beginning now and continuing until God's eternal plan is fulfilled. The Supper celebrates an authentic spiritual union—a critical appropriation of Christ's life that is to be re-enacted and remembered—by which the followers proclaim its efficacy until the God-sent Redeemer returns. All this carries the marks of a Greco-Asian hunger to be purified by divine cleansing, to be marked and prepared for the afterlife, and to be infused with the life-sustaining power of the deity through ritually ingesting the god's flesh and blood. Paul turned these grizzly effects of a general in-God mysticism into a specific in-Christ mystical experience, combining this with the power of transcendence to re-ennoble human life in a manner similar to Israel's own re-enactment of its historical deliverance from bondage through the celebration of Passover. Otherwise, the ingestion of bread and wine as symbols of Jesus' *flesh and blood* make no sense in terms of Judaism's biblical past. The act would have been repugnant to that tradition, but possibly less so to Paul and even lesser to John.

In the Greco-Asian region, the above was honored and practiced. From the time of the Eleusinian Mysteries, the Eastern regions of Asia were drawn to myriad cultic events. Among the more popular were the cult of Dionysus and his followers; the mysteries pertaining to Demeter, Persephone, and Hades; the Egyptian

3. Paul of Tarsus and His Knowledge of Jesus

rites associated with Isis, Osiris, and Horus; and the Orphic cult as well as the Ba'al rituals and the horrific rites governing Attis and Cybele. Of especial interest are the intriguing ramifications of the "communion rites" associated with Demeter's cult. Eating a loaf of grain and drinking wine was associated with celebrating Persephone's release from Hades. Since the cult revolved around agricultural cycles, its celebration was repeated each spring to assure Persephone's return. Or, as Paul explains in reference to the Lord's Supper, "you do proclaim the Lord's death until his return." Traditional Pauline studies account for the latter on the basis of Paul's eschatological views, but the frequency of celebrating the Lord's Supper as Paul commends it is nonetheless a facet of the Hellenistic mind-set concerning the importance of the commemoration of annual renewal rites.

These mysteries provided immense spiritual encouragement to those who practiced them. Meaningfulness, peace, and the assurance of an afterlife awaited the faithful. Paul would have been familiar with these cults and no doubt repulsed by their grosser features and literal interpretations. Aware of all humanity's need to become new creations, he could understand their misled visions while still cognizant of the cults' similarities with Jesus' death and resurrection as well as with the elements of his Last Supper. Nevertheless, how any of this was to be reconciled with Jewish Scriptures remains a viable question.

This brings us to an investigation of Paul's use of the Septuagint.

By the time we come to Paul's letters—Galatians or 1 Thessalonians, whichever epistle was first—Paul had already achieved a theological synthesis of sorts, though not in the form of dogma. I say "of sorts," inasmuch as Paul shaped his messages in accordance with each community's needs. Only occasionally does he repeat his message's principal themes. Nonetheless, the central tenets of what to make of the historical Jesus were clear in his mind. After all, Paul had been mulling and reshaping them since his Arabia hiatus, as well as proclaiming them for over eleven years. What were these tenets? That Jesus was God's "Son," sent to fulfill the ancient promise made to Abraham, who by means of his faith was deemed "righteous" before God. Now, through Christ's death and resurrection, this righteousness pertains to all who, by their faith in Christ, qualify to become Abraham's offspring—whether Jew or Gentile, male or female, slave or free person. Since the Law enjoined death for the unrighteous, God's heaven-sent Son paid that penalty, thus justifying all who accept him, inasmuch as his crucifixion represents theirs. The latter was an act of atonement, which came at a high cost. What solidifies the truth behind Jesus' cross is the resurrection—the "fact" that *God* raised him from the dead—not that Jesus was immortal, thus manifesting that the Galilean Jesus was God's "Son," his "Suffering Servant," and "Savior [*soter*]" of the world.

Paul's introductory paragraph to the Romans hones his message even further:

> Paul, set apart for the gospel of God, which he promised beforehand through his prophets in the holy scriptures, the gospel concerning his Son, who was descended from David according to the flesh, and was *declared to be Son of God* with power according to the spirit of holiness by resurrection from the dead, Jesus Christ our Lord, through whom we have received grace . . . to bring about the obedience of faith among all the Gentiles. (Rom 1:1–5)

This is specifically why Paul considers his mission's central task to "know nothing but Christ and him crucified" (1 Cor 2:2). Moreover, his obligation is not to the house of Israel, nor to the Jewish nation of the Diaspora, but rather to the Gentiles who are now also Abraham's spiritual offspring. The God of Abraham, who alone is God, welcomes all humankind in Christ. In him, the grace of the Living, Personal, and Sole Transcendent Reality of the Universe has come down to indwell and cleanse, empower and ennoble the individual—everywhere. All that is old is past; all persons may become new creations. Its primary requirement is a leap of faith, which the Gentiles are urged to make.

As Paul "perfected" his message, where in the Septuagint did he find support, proof, inspiration, or justification for his views?

3. Paul of Tarsus and His Knowledge of Jesus

Moreover, to what extent did the early church's acceptance of Jesus as the Promised One influence Paul's selection of the Septuagint's material that appeared most applicable? Simply citing verses from the Septuagint belies the complicated interplay between Jesus' historical life and his followers' emerging conviction that he must have been the Messiah. It all likelihood, it is the latter development that sent his followers back to their Scriptures to justify their convictions. Luke's Gospel clearly indicates that this process occurred. We find it best preserved in the Emmaus Road story and the Stranger's methodology of "beginning with Moses and all the prophets, he [the unrecognized Jesus] interpreted to them the things about himself in all the scriptures" (Luke 24:27). Then, it is only after the Stranger and his hosts arrive at the latter's home that he is *suddenly* revealed to them in *the breaking of the bread*—suggesting that the breaking of the bread was already an established memorial celebration whose theological meaning was still in the process of being developed.

Of the supporting Septuagint texts that Paul "cites," few equal in importance to his allusions to Isa 55:5–12 and Hos 6:3. They appear in 1 Cor 15:3–4, where Paul writes: "For I handed on to you as of first importance what I in turn received: that Christ died for our sins in accordance with the scriptures, and that he was buried, and that he was raised on the third day in accordance with the scriptures." It is Isaiah's passage that alludes to the suffering, death, and burial of Israel's Suffering Servant, while Hos 6:3 associates God's deliverance of Israel on "the third day." The Septuagint translated the Isaiah-Hebrew text as follows:

> He bears our sins, and is pained for us; . . . in suffering and affliction. But he was wounded on account of our sins, and was bruised because of our iniquities: the chastisement of our peace was upon him; and by his bruises we were healed . . . The LORD also is pleased to take away from the travail of his soul, to shew him light, and to form him with understanding; to justify the just one who serves many well; and he shall bear their sins. Therefore, he shall inherit many, and he shall divide the spoils of the mighty; because his soul was delivered to death: and

he was numbered among the many, and was delivered because of their iniquities ... and the LORD gave him up for our sins (Isaiah 53:4-6; 11-12, Gr.).[5]

As for the "third day," the allusion is less specific. In context, it refers to God's forbearance of the Ten Northern Tribes once they return to God. "After two days he will heal us: in the third day we shall arise, and live before him, and shall know him (Hosea 6:3, Gr)."[6]

It is clear that the early Jesus movement not only found these passages reassuring, but also illuminating as they struggled with the realities of Jesus' life. That the "tradition" Paul cites is similar to the early community's emerging *kerygma* (Acts 2:14-36) also attests to the widespread process of searching the Septuagint for clues that might shed light on the historical Jesus' life, purpose, and death.

This process not only underlies the quest to understand Jesus' death and reports of his resurrection, it also became an instrumental facet behind Paul's doctrine of justification by faith alone—an insight he based on passages in Genesis. In fact, Bornkamm considered Paul's emphasis on "the Christian gospel as the gospel of justification by faith alone" to be Paul's unique contribution to the movement, which went beyond anything the Jerusalem *kerygma* knew.[7] For example, throughout his Letter to the Galatians, it is Abraham's belief in God's promise that constitutes the Patriarch's "righteousness" (Gen 15:6). Paul cites this text in Gal 3:8 as well as similar texts from Gen 12:3 and 18:18. Paul utilizes these references again, along with Hab 2:4, in his Letter to the Romans, deemed by many as his most definitive epistle.

Paul will draw upon the Scriptures of the Septuagint to illuminate other subjects that his missionary journeys required him to address, but concerning what to make of Jesus' crucifixion and resurrection, the Genesis texts provided Paul with the major scriptural interpretation he needed to establish his doctrine of justification by grace through faith. Whatever anyone else was saying, his

---

5. Brenton, *Septuagint*, 889.
6. Ibid., 1074.
7. Bornkamm, *Paul*, 237.

3. Paul of Tarsus and His Knowledge of Jesus

conscience required him to found his thoughts on the best biblical foundation possible. Nevertheless, the most important development that contributed to Paul's spiritual consciousness is inseparable from his personal "ontological revelations" (whether in the form of *apocalypsis* or *ophthé*), along with his periods of reflection in Arabia and in his homeland of Cilicia. What exactly might the above have entailed?

We know that immediately following his persecution of members of the Jesus movement, Paul experienced an *apocalypsis* that transformed his life. Luke describes it in gripping detail, referring to it no less than three times and twice depicting Paul as retelling it himself in defense at his trials. Paul, however, makes no such claim, reporting in 1 Cor 15:8 only that "as to one untimely born, he [the risen Jesus] appeared [*ophthé*] also to me." To this date, no one can say with certainty what this "revelation" contained, but Paul refers to it again twice in Galatians, thanking God that it pleased him "to reveal his Son to me," whereupon later he went up to Jerusalem "in response to a revelation" to confer with the Jerusalem fathers. This second "revelation" appears to mean nothing more than Paul's realization that he needed to confer with the Jerusalem home church. The other "revelation" remains a mystery too personal and beyond words for Paul to describe. One can only speculate as to its content, but it was powerful enough to be life transforming, however noetic or mystical.

It is possible that Paul's conscience began to affect him as he persecuted members of the Jesus "sect"—as he would have considered it. Did not their faith in one hanged on a "tree" degrade them enough? Thank God the Romans allowed his people the right to extradite offenders who threatened the heart of his people's faith. Yet were not all humankind, all *beni-ha-atham*, whether Jew or Gentile, male or female, slave or free, "children of God"? The latter thought certainly haunted Paul (Gal 3:28) enough for it to become the universal principle behind God's promise of righteousness to all Abraham's offspring. Did his own role in the hunting down of the followers of the Way trouble him now? What if that "accursed one on his tree" (Lev 18:5; Deut 21;23) was the Servant who "was wounded on account of... sins" (Isa 53, Gr.)? The tree, the cross, his wounds, his afflictions? Did Paul slow his gait? Did his conscience balk as he galloped along toward Damascus?

"Why are you persecuting me?" he could imagine the Servant whispering. "Why are you kicking against the goads?" *Why?* Paul wondered. *Yes, why?* Blindness filled his mind.

"Can someone help me?" Paul might well have asked.

"Yes," a voice from someone in Paul's retinue would have answered. "There are followers ahead in Damascus." And so he went on, first to Damascus and then to Arabia.

How long Paul stayed in Arabia is still unknown. Speculation places his "retreat" in the environs of Petra. Founded sometime during the early Hellenistic era, the site itself was ancient. In the center of its plateau, surrounded by steep, pink-red mountains, legend located a still more ancient site atop a central rise where Aaron was reputed to have offered sacrifices to God. Might Paul have climbed its heights and pondered the whole Israelite system of sacrifice and atonement vis-à-vis the person of Jesus, whose death and alleged resurrection now commanded his attention? Did it serve as a background of the unfolding "revelations" that more and more were "opening" Paul's mind to the possibility? It is doubtful that Petra housed a library for its more educated citizens to read, least of all one containing scrolls of the Septuagint, although that supposition is not entirely unfeasible. In any event, Paul's stay in Arabia provided sufficient time to reflect on his Hebrew heritage and the tumultuous events revolving around the emergence of the followers of the Way. One cannot help but suspect that it was in this setting that the rudiments of Paul's thoughts congealed to give rise to his specific insight: that Jesus was the heaven-sent Redeemer, the Promised One, the true "offspring" through which the nations of the earth would be blessed and through whom, by faith, his followers would become "righteous." If that were so, then the era of Jeremiah's new covenant (Jer 31:31) had dawned. The old had passed away, along with the requirements of the Law—the era of salvation by grace through faith was at hand.

3. Paul of Tarsus and His Knowledge of Jesus

Paul collected his sparse belongings, perhaps toured the ancient site once more, strolling through its marketplace and its amphitheater of rose-pink stone before surveying its recessed temples in the rugged mountains, then saddling what mount he could afford and heading for Damascus and "home." Paul was ready to commit his life to the liberating presence and power of Christ Jesus and to the meaning of his death and resurrection. It all seemed to fit in with Paul's new understanding of what he had heard from others and of what to make of his own personal "self-encounter" with the Transcendent Christ—and all of it in the light of his people's revered Scriptures. It was time to get on with his life.

Finally, and not to be neglected, was Paul's conviction that the rabbinical casuistry in which he had been nurtured was no longer applicable. Its emphasis on days and moons, eating, separating oneself from Gentiles (including presumably the washing of hands), foods offered to gods or not, and, above all, the requirement and rite of circumcision—all forms and rituals of a Torah casuistry—had served *at best* only in an ancillary capacity until Christ could come. All now were no longer obligatory for a Christian life. In fact, the Law itself had been surpassed, though it had served as a faithful disciplinarian until Christ's coming changed the calculus.

Numerous passages surface in Paul's letter marking his attitude toward the Law. One might even wonder at the extent to which this development is more attributable to Paul than anyone else in the early church. Certainly Jesus retained respect for the Law, seeing his own mission as advancing its fulfillment as part of the kingdom's goal (Matt 5:17-20). As for the "Tradition of the Elders," however, as a tradition that was non-binding in Jesus' view, Paul favored its rejection (Mark 7:1-16).

For Paul, the central purpose of the Law had nothing to do with the casuistic addenda that they had inherited; rather, it had to do with God's promise to Abraham until the Messiah should come. Moreover, according to Schweitzer, Paul held the view that the Law was not really the work of God but instead contained the ordinances of the angels to whom God had given the governance of the world. Or at least the Law, if stemming from God, had been transmitted through the angels to God's people, Israel. Schweitzer finds adequate evidence in support of his claim.

Writes Schweitzer: "Paul strangely imports a view peculiar to himself, namely, that the Law was given by Angels who desired thereby to make men subservient to themselves." Upon Christ's death, however, the angels lost their power and thus their hold over humankind. As Schweitzer explains, "In Late Judaism in general God is conceived as being so transcendent that any direct contact with men becomes difficult to imagine."[8] Stephen asserts as much in Acts 7:38 and 53. The same view is supported in Heb 2:2 and equally endorsed by Josephus in his *Antiquities of the Jews* 15.5.3. In the latter, Josephus reports that Herod inspired his soldiers before a battle against Arabs by reminding them that God had blessed their nation with sacred laws delivered by none other than God's holy angels. Schweitzer goes on to cite the book of Jubilees (1:27–2:2 and elsewhere), as well as the Septuagint version of Deut 33:2, wherein God's angels are the attendants of the giving of the Law. Even Paul attests as much in Gal 3:19, stating: "Why then the law? It was added because of transgressions, until the offspring would come to whom the promise had been made; and it was ordained through angels by a mediator"—namely, Christ. In the Leviticus chapter (26:46) on which Paul bases this claim, however, the mediator is Moses, whom Paul refers to in Greek as a *mesités*—an acceptable term in Paul's time for Moses meaning the negotiator between God and man.[9] Of what value now was the Law that brought humankind such a curse, as well as the continued observance of moons and days, seasons, foods, Sabbaths, ceremonies, and circumcision, other than retaining the Lord's Supper and the symbolic cleansing and rising to new life that baptism signified and celebrated? One can grasp, then, why Paul so passionately accepted his "call" to preach the gospel of Christ "and him crucified" and nothing more.

---

8. Schweitzer, *Mysticism of Paul*, 68–70.
9. Ibid.

4. Pillar Two: The Consolation of Mysticism

Paul was a "mystic," though hardly a cenobite. He was an apostle imbued with a profound consciousness of the mystical Other. This is demonstrable in spite of what modern Pauline scholarship insists to the contrary. Paul found consolation in frequent moments of ecstatic experience—to which he often alludes—that played a major role in shaping his life and thought. To that degree, his mysticism was authentic, as difficult as that may be for some interpreters to accept. Schweitzer was correct, if not justified, in assigning the term "mystical" to Paul's personality as well as to his outlook, viewing it as an inseparable facet of the apostle's sense of transcendence—that he belonged to another and not to himself. As in the case of the major assumptions that informed the views of Paul's era, so too its "mysticism" shaped his personal and religious convictions.

In his study of Hellenistic mysticism, Luther Martin of the University of Vermont notes that a critical shift occurred between the late Classical era and the rise of the Hellenistic period. In the former, the sacred order of things was deemed to be "immanent in a particular terrestrial realm or locale," such as Zeus and his Olympians, whose holy site was Mount Olympus, and from whose realm Zeus ruled the earth, Poseidon the sea, and Hades the underworld. It was an era founded on piety, ritual, and symbol in order to address the "problematic nature of an existence ruled by [fate],"[1] which Homer's *Iliad* and the tragedies of Aeschylus, Sophocles, and Euripides so powerfully attest. As time passed, this

---

1. Martin, *Hellenistic Religions*, 59.

order was shaken, most notably by the rise of Alexander's conquests and the demise of the city-state as a socio-political-religious organizing principle. The rise of the Roman Empire completed the change. The appeal of local gods and their ability to speak to the human condition waned; thus, the older framework of traditional piety was replaced by cults attuned to newer epiphanies of gods and goddesses who were deemed better able to offer the individual personal fulfillment. In the myths of these new mysteries, the old gods were exchanged for a new set of wandering gods and heroes, goddesses and heroines, whose trials and sufferings (especially in the case of Dionysus) led eventually to a transformed status and ascendance as celestial deities. What happened to them could now happen to a believer, including catharsis, ecstasy, cleansing, and even experiencing an out-of-body reunification with the divine.[2] Paul's letters clearly indicate that he experienced such moments of catharsis and ecstasy in which Christ became his epiphany and manifestation of the divine.

Before examining these, however, an analysis of what mysticism involves is central to our subject because it illuminates Paul's mystical experiences and whether they were similar to or dissimilar to the mystery cults about him. We have already touched on Schweitzer's views, but other perspectives are also relevant. Specifically, Rudolf Otto's definition of "mysticism" is worth reviewing. Not all of Otto's insights apply, but many do. Writes Otto:

> We come upon the ideas, first, of the annihilation of self, and then, as its complement, of the transcendent as the sole and entire reality. These are the characteristic notes of mysticism in all its forms . . . For one of the chiefest and most general features of mysticism is just this self-deprecation, . . . the estimation of the self, of the personal "I" as something not perfectly or essentially real, or even as mere nullity, a self-depreciation which comes to demand its own fulfillment in practice in rejecting the delusion of selfhood, and so makes for the annihilation of the self. And on the other hand mysticism leads to a valuation of the transcendent object of its reference as

2. Ibid., 62.

4. Pillar Two: The Consolation of Mysticism

that which thorough plenitude of being stands supreme and absolute, so that the finite self contrasted with it becomes conscious even in its nullity that "I am naught, Thou art all."[3]

For Otto, mysticism is the overstressing "of the non-rational or supra-rational elements in religion, thus resulting in feelings of 'littleness' and the exaltation of 'creaturehood' over human 'createdness.'"[4] That Otto's analysis sheds light on Paul's experiences is undeniable. However, the degree to which Paul embraced his "littleness," or Otto's "nullity" or "self deprecation," over against the power of the Holy Spirit to transform his life, remains in question. The latter is true inasmuch as, rather than luxuriating in a full, mystical, spiritual, and anchorite withdrawal from the world, Paul's mystical experiences sent him back into the world, filled with a zealous effort to "convert" as many followers as he could. By preaching Christ only, "and him crucified," Paul's mysticism provided an urgency and consolation that the mystery cults could not match.

If there is one central mystical element that underlies Paul's theology, it is surely grounded in the revelation(s) to which he often returns and cites. He tells us twice (1 Cor 9:1; 1 Cor 15:8) that he "saw" (*ophthé*) the risen Jesus, but whether in Christ's "imperishable" form or "spiritual body," Paul does not clarify. Whichever it was, Paul's claim is rooted nonetheless in the "non-rational" or "supra-rational" elements that haunt all mystical encounters with the numinous and transcendent, or Otto's "Wholly other." Instead of experiencing the "dread," or "fear," or "awefulness [sic]" that Otto associates with transcendence, Paul experiences a liberation from "fear and dread," a resonance, a raison d'être that floods his existentiality with zeal and consolation.

This is not to say that Paul's "revelation" (*apokalypsis*) or "revelations" did not contain elements of "dread" and "awe" or a life-long sense of wonder, remorse, and guilt. Paul's persecution of the followers of the Way ever remained a facet of his consciousness.

3. Otto, *Idea of the Holy*, 21.
4. Ibid., 22.

In that sense, he carried his acknowledged shame to the end of his life, but the surpassing knowledge of Christ Jesus' death and resurrection (which clearly contained the *rational content* of his revelations—however *ecstatic* their intensity) is what lifted Paul above any daily sense of absolute worthlessness. Nor did Paul's "revelations" quench his feelings of awe and majesty before God. One of his more notable passages to this effect is found in Paul's Letter to the Philippians. There, after reviewing the "self-emptying" of Christ, Paul urges his readers to "work out their own salvation with fear and trembling," inasmuch as it is God who is at work in them (Phil 2:12–13). Paul honored the otherness of God that cost God the death of his Son.

If we turn to Karen Armstrong's *A History of God*, we find a similar, yet different definition of mysticism. For Armstrong, the "mystical experience of God has certain characteristics that are common to all faiths." She lists three: "[1] a subjective experience that involves an interior journey, not a perception of an objective fact outside the self; [2] it is undertaken through the image-making part of the mind . . . Finally, [3] it is something that the mystic creates in himself or herself deliberately."[5] Her definition constitutes a critical insight with respect to Paul. That Paul's mystical experiences are highly subjective is beyond doubt. As we shall see, they ranged from quiet reflection to intense feelings of celestial joy—an interior journey, yes, yet one that recognized the objectivity of God as higher than Paul's subjectivity. Still, it is feasible to conclude, as Armstrong's definition suggests, that Paul himself created his interior world in which the Jesus of history became the divine Mediator between God and humankind. To that extent, Paul's Christ Jesus is a construct of his subjectivity. This set Paul apart from the other apostles, bolstered his sense of authority, and contributed to the vision of Christ that enabled Paul to establish, if not radically influence, the form of Christianity that took wing after his death.

Paul's letters confirm with engaging detail the degree to which his subjective experiences, or spiritual mysticism, deepened his life. It is paramount throughout his work. For example, 2 Cor

---

5. Armstrong, *History of God*, 219.

4. Pillar Two: The Consolation of Mysticism

4:18 and 5:6–15 capture a number of qualitative ways in which Paul's mystical leanings, guided by rational reflection, influenced his work. In one of Paul's most Platonic passages, he notes: "So we do not lose heart. Even though our outer nature is wasting away, our inner nature is being renewed day by day . . . because we look not at what can be seen but at what cannot be seen; for what can be seen is temporary, but what cannot be seen is eternal" (2 Cor 4:16–18). Or, again, "So we are always confident; even though we know that while we are at home in the body we are away from the LORD . . . [as] we would rather be away from the body and at home with the LORD." If that appeared unsettling to the Corinthians, Paul went on to explain: "For if we are beside ourselves [*exéstamen*, or "ecstatic"], it is for God; if we are in our right mind [*sophronoumen*, or "soundness of mind"], it is for you" (2 Cor 5:13).

Paul continues in this mode by appealing to the ecstatic revelations of "a person in Christ who fourteen years ago was caught up to the third heaven" (whether in or out of the body, he doesn't know), in which the person was taken "up into Paradise and heard things that are not to be told, that no mortal is permitted to repeat" (2 Cor 12:2–4). Paul could boast of these but preferred not to, "even considering the exceptional character of the revelations." That he was referring to himself is indeed likely, as Paul concludes the report by stating that, lest he remain too elated, God inflicted him with a "thorn in the flesh" in order to teach him that God's grace alone was sufficient, insofar as God's "power is made perfect in weakness" (2 Cor 12:9).

Further nuances of Paul's mystical views emerge even more clearly in his anticipation of the resurrection that all Christians are promised to enjoy. He speaks glowingly of the imperishable body that awaits believers at the end time. His vision of this "event" as explained in 1 Cor 15:50–58 provides one of the most vivid objectifications of Paul's inward spiritual state found anywhere in his collection.

"Listen, I will tell you a mystery! We will not all die, but we will be changed, in a moment, in the twinkling of an eye, at the last trumpet. For the trumpet will sound, and the dead will be raised imperishable" (1 Cor 15:51–52). More tellingly, Paul prefaces this vision with an even more succinct explanation found in 15:20–25. Interlacing the power of the Universal with its salvific effects upon the particular, Paul explains how Christ's death and resurrection now pertain to all believing individuals. Writes Paul: "Since death came through a human being, the resurrection of the dead has also come through a human being; for as all die in Adam, so all will be made alive in Christ." Nonetheless, an orderly succession must transpire. First Christ is raised, then his followers, then comes the End, "when he hands over the kingdom to God the Father; after he has destroyed every ruler and every authority and power" (1 Cor 15:25). Paul narrates this same series of events in 1 Thess 4:16–17 in an equally ecstatic mystical vision: "For the LORD himself, with a cry of command, with the archangel's call and with the sound of God's trumpet, will descend from heaven, and the dead in Christ will rise first. Then we who are alive, who are left, will be caught up in the clouds together with them to meet the LORD in the air; and so we will be with the LORD forever." Such mystical insights obviously contributed to Paul's interpretation of the ultimate significance of the historical Jesus, who was now deemed God's Son and Messiah by virtue of his resurrection.

There are additional passages worth citing too, particularly in 1 Corinthians, where Paul delineates between the *wisdom of the present age* and the *spiritual wisdom of God*, reflected specifically in the scandal of the cross. As we might expect, Paul insists that God's wisdom transcends the wisdom of the world and can be grasped only by a *consciousness inspired by God's spirit alone*. It is a wisdom made available through spiritual consciousness, if not the mystical indwelling of God's Spirit. As Paul explains:

> But we speak God's wisdom [*theou sophian*], secret and hidden, which God decreed before the ages for our glory. None of the rulers of this age understood this; for if they had, they would not have crucified the Lord of glory. But as it is written: "What no eye has seen, nor ear heard, nor the human heart conceived, what God has prepared for those who love him"—these things God has

4. Pillar Two: The Consolation of Mysticism

revealed to us through the Spirit; for the Spirit searches everything, even the depths of God . . . Now we have received not the spirit of the world, but the Spirit that is from God, so that we may understand the gifts bestowed on us by God. (1 Cor 2:7–12)

No clearer passage could be cited to demonstrate Paul's reliance on grasping what the "mystical eye of faith" alone can apprehend, provided the Spirit of God awakens it and stirs it to comprehend what heretofore has been "secret and hidden" (*mystério, tan apokekprymmenan*).

Paul goes on to boast of further gifts, especially of his personal gift of tongues, though he prefers not to exalt himself or enlarge upon his unique experiences. Still, he writes, "I thank God that I speak in tongues more than all of you" (1 Cor 14:18). In his favor, however, Paul refuses to allow this particular ecstatic gift to detract from his real "call," which is to proclaim the liberating power of the cross. To that extent, Bornkamm is right to insist that Paul never championed any "individual subjective religious experience" as a norm for others, even if it was for himself.[6] What emerges is something in the way of a mystical orientation initiated by Paul's revelations, which inspired a motivation to seek the spiritual edification of Christ's followers everywhere.

For himself, Paul's mystical experiences provided a threefold path to the fulfillment of his personal identity: (1) by affording him ontological wholeness, as well as (2) a perspicuity that transcended and addressed the incongruities of existence, resulting in (3) an ethic of liberating imperatives that were capable of rehumanizing life. Since we cannot exchange our mental world for the mystical world of Paul's, we can at least appreciate its hopes and yearnings as reflective of our own. The threefold satisfaction that Paul's hiddenness in Christ brought him is a consolation that modern humanity can equally appropriate in its own quest for ontological wholeness. The key, however, as obvious as it may seem, is far from simple, for how we define the spiritual content of that "hiddenness" determines everything.

6. Bornkamm, *Paul*, 189.

Transcendence and Fulfilment

Few philosophers address ontological wholeness in our time, but its importance cannot be stressed enough. Fortunately for Paul, both his Asian and Hebraic heritage offered approaches to attain such wholeness. We have already mentioned a trio of assumptions that guided the process, but other avenues remained intact in Paul's time. Let us reflect on the more historical and their relevance for us.

Paul's Jewish heritage had already planted seeds of awareness of one's ontological identification with God, though hardly expressed in philosophical language. "What are human beings that you are mindful of them?" (Ps 8:4) is one of the most insightful passages in religious literature that probes the human situation. If ontological wholeness means anything, it means that humankind longs for a self-understanding that can do justice to the mystery of its being: Why am I here? For what purpose do I exist? What happens to me once my being passes away? Have I been born simply to exist, to live life to its end, and nothing more? Is Being itself without a Ground, without any ultimate reason or purpose for existing other than existence itself? Is that the essence of the human condition? That we are born into the world without reason or purpose and that our unique individuality has no destiny, no carry over, no remainder or value? That we are slated to pass away into the vacuous category of Non-being, which itself will be swallowed up once the bright stars and glowing galaxies of the universe become dying embers against an eternal dark?

Tillich referred to the above as a central aspect of the human condition, identifying it as the "fear of non-being."[7] If there is no Ground of Being that is the ultimate ground of one's own being, then there exists no ontological wholeness in any absolute sense. Or, as Tillich states repeatedly throughout his work, "God is the answer to the question implied in human finitude."[8] Without God, we would be reliant on our own powers to affirm our being, which in itself is a form of transcendence. To that extent, transcendence is inescapable. We cannot help but ask why and long for some

---

7. Tillich, *Systematic*, 64–67.
8. Ibid., 64–65.

4. Pillar Two: The Consolation of Mysticism

stabilizing principle that gives our lives their sense of worth. That God exists is the highest spiritual form of transcendence, addressing our fear of being forgotten while equally granting our lives ultimate worth. Indeed, the phenomenon of mystical union that accompanies transcendence—to whatever degree of intensity, for however long—still nurtures the human heart.

It is what Plato meant by his idea of the Good—that eternal, unbegotten, wholly other transcendence—that alone lifts humankind above the physical realm of disparate distractions and human sorrow. His was as much a mystical view as was Paul's, a construct of his interior world that united him with the highest Good and the highest degree of Being he could imagine. From a theological perspective, only when that is incarnated in one's life may one say with Paul, "It is no longer I who live, but the highest transcendence knowable that dwells in me." It is why Socrates, along with Plato, still appeals to our philosophical restlessness, and it is why we find Aristotle's *Nicomachean Ethics* to be of continuing relevance. To experience transcendence in any form that results in a relationship with that which is "higher," at whatever ontological, mystical, cognitive, or historical level, is worth retaining.

In our own time, the philosopher Heidegger embraced this vision in his uniquely demanding way, at least with respect to transcendence. Many have found his views obscure but relevant nonetheless.

In his inaugural work, *Existence and Being*, Heidegger set out to create a bold new program for reassessing the meaning of one's being. His views are too extensive to do justice in any in-depth way here, but a brief summary of their relationship to transcendence is germane. For Heidegger, we find ourselves "thrown" into the world with little preparation for knowing what to do. It is a characteristic of our *Dasein*, of our being-here, of what-is, with all its possibilities and limitations, or what Heidegger calls "the totality of what-is." That we are mortal and will die, that our span of life is unique and its length unknown, adds to this facticity. It creates a mood of dread and uncertainty that one has to address. If one fails to address it, then one forfeits one's unique opportunity to surmount life's encroachments, and one thus falls into inauthenticity. *Dasein*, facticity, the potential for forfeiture, and the dread of losing authenticity ever gnaw at the human conscience, along with its consciousness of past, present, and future. This is the human condition, like it or not. But the positive side of this ledger lies in its capacity to initiate a longing for a solution, for a metaphysics that can overcome one's sense of abandonment and result in the attainment of an authentic existence. Of such is the role and value of metaphysics, if not of transcendence.

For Heidegger, however, transcendence comes with a risk. It involves a disturbing and anxious leap into the sphere of Nothingness, as ontological a state as it is psychological. Nothingness is the form of that "ontological dread" that brings one to the question of just what is one's status and place in the midst of "what-is." Nothingness is a cipher as well, a metaphor for humankind's searching for just what one's being means or can become. Thus, through one's searching for joy and happiness—for that which lies beyond dread—one is brought face-to-face with Nothingness, or "the complete negation of the totality of what-is."[9] Yet at the same time, one is brought to the possibility of discovering one's true Being (*Sein*), which for Heidegger is what transcendence means:

"This projection into Nothing on the basis of hidden dread is the overcoming of what-is-in-totality: Transcendence."[10] Thus, "Nothing is that which makes the revelation of what-is as such possible for our human existence." And it is "in the Being (*Sein*) of what-is that the nihilation of Nothing (*das Nichten des Nichts*) occurs."[11]

Heidegger's above reflections are from his essay "What Is Metaphysics?" in his *Existence and Being*. In concluding his essay, Heidegger sought to make his contribution as constructive as possible. Because the fear of Nothingness forces us to put our lives to the question, it is a "wonder" to be appreciated and a doorway to true authenticity. Heidegger does not say how it will come out, but

---

9. Heidegger, *Existence and Being*, 436.
10. Ibid., 441.
11. Ibid., 439.

4. Pillar Two: The Consolation of Mysticism

it is a welcome task for metaphysics to ponder, though any final answer lies beyond metaphysics itself. This is where religion enters with its own metaphorical solution to the question of being. In a powerful appeal for humankind never to abandon the role that philosophy plays, Heidegger writes:

> Philosophy is only set in motion by leaping with all its being . . . into the ground-possibilities of being as a whole. For this leap the following things are of crucial importance: firstly, leaving room for what-is-in-totality; secondly, letting oneself go into Nothing, that is to say, freeing oneself from the idols we all have and to which we are wont to go cringing; lastly, letting this "suspense" range where it will . . .[12]

Heidegger's concept of transcendence constitutes a vision that any human being can find reasonable, latent with the potential to transform one's life for the better.

In closing this section, it is helpful to remember that Paul belonged to an era in which omens and ecstatic trances were not uncommon elements of divination and the quest for authenticity. One only has to read Plutarch's *Parallel Lives* to realize the mesmerizing hold that trances and the occult played on Greco-Roman imaginations. Plutarch's description of the conception of the future ruler Alexander combines fantasy with myth in a breathtaking narrative of how his mother, Olympias, became pregnant. It holds in common something of an untamed replication of Luke's own story of the Angel Gabriel's announcement of how the Holy Spirit will "overshadow" Mary such that the child she conceives will be "Holy."

Cicero's own appeal to the veracity of tested "myth" also comes to mind. In his essay "On the Commonwealth," Cicero makes a telling point with respect to the founding of Rome. He argues that until the time of Romulus, the older myths of Greece and Rome lacked believability and failed to inspire humankind. But with the coming of Romulus and the more historical nuances associated with his birth, upbringing, exploits, and trials, the legends

---

12. Ibid., 443.

Transcendence and Fulfilment

supporting his story and ascendance into heaven were deemed believable.[13]

Elements of myth and fantasy, miracle and voices, visions and revelations were simply popular forms for creating a genre of fascinating literature for the period. Luke, more so than any of the other gospel writers, adapted this approach. In Acts alone, there are over thirty references to signs and wonders (*dynameis*), visions (*orama*), trances (*ecstasei*), voices (*phoné*), the Angel of the Lord (*aggelos de Kuriou*), and other miraculous signs. In comparison, Paul's ecstatic revelations, disclosures, and paradisiacal ascents are actually minimal, if not reported with sensitivity so as not to offend those for whom such experiences may likely never occur.

Mystical experiences—or feelings of being strangely at one with the universe—are legitimate spiritual occasions, as worthy and hungered for today as ever. The notion that our minds and bodies carry remnants of the big bang—something of that Kabbalistic belief in the glowing shards of God's glory still pulsating in the universe—fills us with ontological wonder and brings the Eternal down into our common lives. That our DNA throbs with the elements that make life possible equally nurtures our awareness of belonging to something vastly beyond our finite moments within the Infinite flow of time's hourglass. Above all, to experience the Infinite as "Thou," as a conscious presence that bonds itself to the mystery of our own existence, fills us with a sense of eternity to which we shall forever belong. It did for Paul, culminating in a consolation that bore him through the inevitable highs and lows of life. As he put it so eloquently for the Philippians, so he would he repeat it for humankind today: "I have learned to be content with whatever I have. I know what it is to have little, and I know what it is to have plenty. In any and all circumstances I have learned the secret of being well fed and of going hungry, of having plenty and of being in need. I can do all things through him who strengthens me" (Phil 4:11–13).

---

13. Cicero, *Commonwealth*, 372.

5. Spiritual Consciousness: Its Depths and Dimensions

Since the late 1990s, a variety of publishing houses have begun reissuing seminal works on mysticism and spirituality. Herder & Herder has taken something of a lead in this movement in its efforts to counter the growing disparity between religion and spirituality—where religion is viewed as rote, authoritarian, and institutional, while spirituality is seen as personal, individualistic, and dogma-free. Herder & Herder has done so by releasing a number of masterworks dedicated to preserving the unity of spiritual life both in its intellectual form and in its "manifestation" in one's personal life. Foremost among these recent publications are Friedrich von Hügel's *The Mystical Element of Religion*, along with other works and studies of past mystics. Likewise, Dover Publications has reissued the original and unabridged first edition of Evelyn Underhill's *Mysticism: A Study in the Nature and Development of Spiritual Consciousness*. Concomitant with the above, Johns Hopkins University Press also republished Albert Schweitzer's 1929 *The Mysticism of Paul the Apostle*, translated by William Montgomery and consulted in all four or this book's chapters above.

The concern these books address is legitimate and recaptures a central aspect of the Christian faith—its spirituality—a matter of importance to other religions as well. In doing so, it provides a safeguard against the soul's enterprise being usurped by a metaphysics that inadvertently substitutes a "philosophy of religion" for the heart's hunger to "know God directly." If anything, spirituality has signaled humanity's longing to experience the Highest Source of Pure *Being*, come down to indwell the individual soul while lifting it up to the realm of divine glory, in one's tested and solitary journey of *becoming*.

Paul's letters amply attest to his own journey, as he sought to appropriate the Living Christ in his heart. Whatever the cost of the journey, Paul refused to be discouraged or led astray by the numerous exigencies he faced. As he writes in 2 Cor 4:1, 5, 7–10, and 16–18, some of which we have quoted before:

> Therefore, since it is by God's mercy that we are engaged in this ministry, we do not lose heart . . . For we do not proclaim ourselves; we proclaim Jesus Christ as Lord and ourselves as your slaves for Jesus' sake . . . But we have this treasure in clay jars, so that it may be made clear that *this extraordinary power belongs to God and does not come from us*. We are afflicted in every way, but not crushed; perplexed, but not driven to despair; persecuted, but not forsaken; struck down, but not destroyed; always carrying in the body the death of Jesus, so that the life of Jesus may also be made visible in our bodies . . . So we do not lose heart. Even *though our outer nature is wasting away, our inner nature is being renewed day by day. For . . . we look not at what can be seen but at what cannot be seen; for what can be seen is temporary, but what cannot be seen is eternal*.

Paul's entire mission is founded on this mystical vision, sustained and empowered by his ontological union with Christ, which nurtured his spiritual consciousness to dare it all. Pauline scholarship cannot denigrate his mystical inner self-consciousness or his perceived ontological union with Christ without compromising the apostle's spiritual depths, let alone his influence on the numerous cluster of tiny ecclesia he founded and risked his life to maintain.

This is why the call of the Transcendent, in its mystical, spiritual, and even ecstatic forms, cannot be totally replaced by an intellectual, cognitive, or rational element alone. Nor even can it be sustained outside a community of like-minded souls without becoming overly self-focused, self-centered, and delusional. We gain nothing enduring from Paul if we eliminate the empowering

5. Spiritual Consciousness: Its Depths and Dimensions

splendor of God's Being in his life, whether experienced mystically in union with Christ or through the accompanying presence of the Holy Spirit, even when infused with ecstatic instances of God's apocalyptic moments of self-disclosure. When that element is taken from Paul—or indeed incised from any religion worldwide—then hearts are left with nothing but the dry bones of propositional statements that inspire no one. That is why the Romantic movement rose up against the Enlightenment, and why the neo-orthodoxy of the past century breathed new life into the staid and rigid corpse of orthodoxy, and also why Nietzsche's Madman was forced to proclaim "the death of God."[1] Religion without its mystical dimension, along with dogma, ecclesia, and ritualism severed from spiritual consciousness, ultimately fails the soul and the soul's hunger to experience the highest fulfillment that the Transcendent invites it to explore.

This constitutes a daunting challenge for modern humanity. Our mind-set isn't "otherworldly" or even "mystically oriented," for the most part. Neither heights nor depths, nor angels nor principalities, nor anything else in our perceived universe either links us with or separates us from the phenomenon of the universe. It is just there—the product of a big bang, and we the products of years of evolution. Yet, in our loneliest self-consciousness, we cannot help but wonder if there might not be more. To the extent that we wonder, the world's attraction to spirituality and religion, to reflection and contemplation, provides a home station for humankind's quest for ontological integrity. But that our wholeness should be in the form of Paul's—or even that of the historical Jesus' oneness with the logos—is doubtful, if not impossible. Nevertheless, the journey of viewing one's acts and will as inseparable from the art of allowing the mystery of Being to infuse itself into the reality of our becoming is as relevant today as it was in Paul's time. This is why Heidegger and Marcel's metaphysical views cannot be jettisoned so quickly, and also why von Hügel's or Underhill's studies of mysticism cannot be brushed aside with indifference.

---

1. Nietzsche, *Gay Science*, 181.

Von Hügel's work is certainly worth revisiting. As a child of the Catholic faith of his time—disillusioned, and yet returning to its fold—he achieved a comprehensive view that illuminates both Paul's themes as well as humankind's hunger for the Eternal. Von Hügel's style, like Underhill's, is stilted, old-fashioned, pseudo-scientific as well as pseudo-empirical, yet focused on the worth of embracing the sacred and the holy. Von Hügel argues that there are three components critical to the wellbeing of religion: the institutional, the intellectual, and the spiritual. Diminish any one of the three, and the life of the spirit is diminished with it. For von Hügel, all three contribute to our sense of wholeness. All carry ontological value; all three are essential to our self-definition. Seeing ourselves through their prism and incorporating their nuances in our lives enriches our existentiality, resulting in the wholeness of our individual personalities.

In his introduction to von Hügel's work, Archbishop Michael Downey summarizes these three components with helpful conciseness. Of the *institutional* element, he notes that von Hügel wanted to show "that the ultimate purpose of a religious institution is to mediate, or communicate, the experience of the sacred, of God."[2] This is important, as it provides support for Christians who are tempted to leave the church and go in alone. Von Hügel was too wed to his own tradition, as well as too spiritually astute, to trust a spirituality that severs itself from "texts, traditions, structures of community and authority which [a traditional] religious institution safe-guards and serves, albeit sometimes quite poorly."[3] Paul certainly would have concurred, as he feared that his pagan converts in the Galatians field, as well as in Corinth, would fall prey to individualized concepts of God's Spirit that were contrary to the "truth" of the gospel as the living Christ had "revealed" it to him. Moreover, there was the early church's "tradition" that also needed to be safeguarded, if not "handed down."

Downey summarizes von Hügel's second component, the *intellectual*, as "based on the human capacity for reasoning, for

2. Von Hügel, *Mystical Element*, xiv.
3. Ibid.

5. Spiritual Consciousness: Its Depths and Dimensions

argument and abstraction, and refers to the critical, speculative, and philosophical dimensions of religion." This element helps clarify one's understanding of God, thus better enabling one to communicate it to others.[4]

The third component is the *mystical*. It involves will and action and draws on the "experiential, intuitive, emotional, and mystical element of religion." In von Hügel's own words, it constitutes that dimension "where religion is rather felt than seen or reasoned about, is loved and lived rather than analyzed, is action and power, rather than either external fact or intellectual verification."[5]

All three elements require "interaction" to form "a cross-pollination" among themselves. As von Hügel says of his own research in a note to its second printing in 1909, "May the very defects of the work help to bring home to the reader this inexhaustible richness of its subject-matter, and so indicate the pre-existence, the super-eminence, [and] the independence of the august object of religion"—namely, "God, the Divine Spirit, [who] is indeed before, within, and after all our truest dignity and deepest disquiet."[6]

At the time he was writing—just prior to World War I—von Hügel identified the three "chief forces of Western Civilization" as reasoning, religion, and science. The first alone is too abstract to coax the will to change its life. It relates to the Universal and Abiding primarily through the pathways of logic and abstraction. It is the second force that witnesses to the phenomenon that moves the will—that is, the intuition, feeling, instinct, and personality, along with the "evanescent" that is so difficult to pin down and define. As for the third force, science, its field is "brute fact and iron law," as von Hügel was wont to characterize it. Unlike the intuitive, science utilizes the tools of mathematics, determinism, and monism (the view that all is a unity) to resolve the issues that confront humankind.

Today, we may assess the above as too quaint and without significant capacity to address what we know psychologically about

---

4. Ibid., xvi.
5. Ibid., 63.
6. Ibid., xxiii.

ourselves or scientifically about our universe, yet von Hügel's divisions are not without merit. The abstract alone has rarely moved the heart, nor do scientific findings necessarily bring peace to a broken and contrite soul; nevertheless, both are necessary to the quest of a sound theology or even an illuminating metaphysics, as they are central to the recognition of the facts of life as they are.

Nonetheless, for von Hügel, it is the personal, the individual, the intuitive, the mystical, and the Transcendent that enriches the hidden and secret depths of one's life. Whatever their form, wherever they prevail—for good or evil—they either lift up and elevate or wear down and destroy the human heart.

In a brief yet incisive section on Paul, von Hügel notes that for all the apostle's intellectual rigor and faithfulness to the "historical constituents" pertaining to Jesus' era, it is "the mystical, interior, and experiential element" that knits together the heart of Paul's insight.[7] Furthermore, when thoroughly understood, one cannot help but characterize religion as "more or less both traditional and individual; both external and internal, both institutional, rational, and volitional."[8] It is imperative for these opposites to coalesce, states von Hügel, or else religion will be unable to (1) achieve accountability to society, or (2) offer reasonable cause for its existence, let alone (3) address the spiritual needs of "interior sustenance and purification."[9] If religion ignores its emotional-experiential component, it risks losing its soul. But if religion separates itself from its institutional and external historical past or forgoes "all approaches to . . . reasoned, intellectual apprehension and systematization," then it risks becoming just another -ism alongside all the others—or still worse, a fanatical and anti-intellectual movement driven by emotion alone.[10] Institutionalism, intellectualism, and mysticism simply go hand in hand.

For von Hügel, it was the late-medieval Cardinal Nicolas of Coes who combined all three. In doing so, he was able to show

7. Ibid., 32.
8. Ibid., 54.
9. Ibid.
10. Ibid., 55.

5. Spiritual Consciousness: Its Depths and Dimensions

the way that modern philosophy might proceed by (1) clinging to external authority, (2) respecting the realm of the intellectual and speculative, and (3) honoring "the constant temper and practice of experimental and Mystical piety."[11] Paul approximated the same in his own way and passed its possibility onto us. More could be said, but a glance at one of von Hügel's more astute contemporaries deserves attention.

Evelyn Underhill read von Hügel's work and followed it with a book of her own: *Mysticism: A Study in the Nature and Development of Spiritual Consciousness*. From the first page of chapter 1 on, she defines mysticism as involving the pursuit of "the unknown world, which lies outside the boundaries of sense." More colorfully, Underhill describes it as the "veiled Isis of Truth," or that "hidden truth which is the object of man's craving."[12] Beginning with a critique of naturalism, she echoes the Platonic view that "the evidence of the senses ... cannot be accepted as evidence of the nature of ultimate reality." For the mystic's goal is "a direct encounter with absolute truth."[13] For this reason, naturalism fails to satisfy the soul. Granted, although idealism in turn also has its limits, it at least perceives that "the destinies of mankind are invariably guided, not by the concrete 'facts' of the sense world, but by concepts which are acknowledged by every one to exist only on the mental plane."[14] Idealism therefore provides "the most sublime theory of Being." But just as naturalism fails the human spirit, so too does idealism.

Hence, the intellectual quest alone for life's highest reality fares little better, ending in "three blind alleys." Underhill categorizes these as (1) accepting the "world of appearance" as "real"; or (2) embracing the theory of idealism, "as beautiful as it is," though it is unable to help us to attain the Absolute; or (3) finding ourselves doomed to accept a hopeless skepticism that leads to cynicism and despair.[15]

11. Ibid., 62.
12. Underhill, *Mysticism*, 3–4.
13. Ibid., 6–8.
14. Ibid., 12.
15. Ibid., 15–16.

For Underhill, it is at this impasse that religious consciousness offers itself as the solution. Once this impasse is recognized, it illuminates the fact "that the supra-sensible is somehow important and real, and is intimately connected with the life of man."[16] This is especially true of pain. That humanity by necessity should and will incur suffering and pain, along with anxiety, anguish, and sorrow, attests all the more to the soul's recognition of disharmony between itself and the natural world, thus nudging it humbly toward "the school of the Supra-sensible." These "sufferings" she describes as "the wings on which man's spirit can best take flight toward the Absolute."[17] Furthermore, humanity's experiences of beauty, truth, and love also point toward the transcendent summit of God, especially as love. It is this movement that ultimately defies philosophical skepticism, leading to peace and harmony.

Turning next to psychology, Underhill probes its depths to reveal the truth behind humankind's craving for the Infinite, with all its power to fulfill human life. Beginning first with a review of the "older school of psychology's" belief in humankind's tripartite nature—mind, will, and emotion—which she acknowledged has value, Underhill deemed it inadequate, since it probes only so far before failing in the end. Reviewing psychoanalysis next, which she applauded for its exploration of the unconscious and focus on the libido and hidden archetypes, Underhill vied for a more personal, positive, and kinder view of the depths of psychoanalysis— one that encourages rather than confounds humankind to seek the Transcendent.

Focusing on the lives of the saints, Underhill found life's positive feelings in the human realm of "experience" itself, of "feelings of energy and action" that lead to "love" and not merely to the "passive knowledge" of one's darker and repressed side. To that extent, psychology's focus on feelings, especially on love and reciprocity, illuminate with greater clarity humankind's hunger for the Absolute, more so than any insight offered by intellectual analysis. It is "intimate communion and contemplation" that fulfills one's inner

16. Ibid., 17–18.
17. Ibid., 19.

5. Spiritual Consciousness: Its Depths and Dimensions

drive, she concludes, rather than "intellectual ambition" without "adoration . . . self-spending . . . [or] the feeling between Knower and Known."[18] As Underhill expounds:

> In the sphere of religion it is now acknowledged that "God known of the heart" gives a better account of the character of our spiritual experience than "God guessed by the brain"; that loving intuition is more fruitful and . . . trustworthy than . . . dialectic proof. One by one the commonplaces of mysticism are thus rediscovered by official science, and given their proper place in the psychology of the spiritual life.[19]

It is this form of passion and longing that opens those doors logic fails to budge. In a flash of rhapsodic prose, she states: "It is the lover, the poet, the mourner, the convert, who [ultimately wins] the privilege of lifting [the] Veil of Isis."[20] Above all, the act of "contemplation" becomes the critical "method of going from one level of consciousness to another." This is why Jesus said to Martha, "Mary has chosen the better part" (Luke 10:42). For Underhill, such devotion and awareness is what constitutes "transcendental consciousness" at its best. She continues, "We know . . . that the personality of man is a far deeper and more mysterious thing than the sum of his conscious feeling, thought, and will," and that the phenomenon we call the Ego "hardly counts in comparison with the deeps of being which it hides." However, it is not the "Unconscious" itself that accounts for the content of transcendence; rather, it is the emergence of a transcendental sense that captures one's field of consciousness, thus opening up "paths which permit the inflow of a larger spiritual life, the perception of a higher reality."[21]

The emergence of this field is what constitutes the mystical grounds on which human beings meet "the Absolute, the germ of . . . real life" and where one enters the realm of timeless being. It is what justifies mysticism, or even forms of asceticism, inasmuch

18. Ibid., 46.
19. Ibid., 47.
20. Ibid., 48.
21. Ibid., 51–53.

as it affirms "that there is an extreme point at which man's nature touches the Absolute" and where one encounters true being "penetrated by the Divine Life which constitutes the underlying reality of things."[22] Such is the essence of the transcendental experience that ultimately brings peace and equilibrium to all else one does. Hence, "contemplation, recollection, and ecstasy" all have a vital role to play in the phenomenon of spiritual consciousness, as does silence before the Eternal. Quoting Meister Eckhart, Underhill brings her investigation of psychology slowly to a close: "The best and noblest way thou mayst come into this Life is by keeping silence and letting God work and speak."[23] Thus, philosophically speaking, Being at last frees humankind from all its forms of alienation, flooding its becoming with wholeness. If this is true of mysticism in general, then we can see why Schweitzer insisted that Paul's form was totally "an in-Christ" mysticism, or else Christ's cross and atoning death would have been in vain.

It is only in chapter 4 that Underhill offers her fourfold assessment of mysticism and its contribution to spiritual consciousness. Her categories not only illuminate Paul's own experiences, they also suggest ways that the human heart today may appropriate God's Spirit of grace:

1. "True mysticism is active and practical." "It is something that the whole self does."

2. "Its aims are wholly transcendental and spiritual." It has no interest in adding to or rearranging anything in the universe. Far from calling one to neglect one's "duty to the many," the mystic's heart "is always set upon the changeless One."

3. "This One is . . . not merely the Reality of all that is, but [the] . . . living and personal Object of Love," drawing one's "whole being homeward, but always under the guidance of the heart."

---

22. Ibid., 55.
23. Ibid., 64.

5. Spiritual Consciousness: Its Depths and Dimensions

4. As such, mysticism results in "a definite state or form of enhanced life," or a living in union with God.[24]

For Underhill, mysticism is not "a philosophy," nor a mere "opinion" about life. Neither is it confined to the "contemplation of Eternity," nor defined as a "pursuit of occult knowledge." Rather, "it is the name of that . . . process which involves the perfect consummation of the Love of God: the achievement here and now of the immortal heritage of man."[25]

Whatever one might think, Underhill's four categories capture something of the essence of Paul's noetic and declarative statements regarding his own quest for fulfillment. Though her categories might not have been Paul's, they nonetheless illuminate our understanding of how and why Christ became Paul's ontological gateway to eternity.

Of additional significance, however, is Underhill's chapter on "Ecstasy and Rapture." More than anything else, it enables us to grasp Paul's ecstatic experiences that constitute a genuine facet of his faith.

Underhill defines "ecstasy" as "an exceptionally favourable state: the one in which man's spirit is caught up to the most immediate union with the divine."[26] It is a state "in which the concentration of interest in the Transcendent is so complete . . . [and so intense] that the subject is more or less entranced, and becomes, for the time of the ecstasy, unconscious of the external world."[27]

In her typical way, Underhill distinguishes between three distinct aspects of ecstatic states: the physical, psychological, and mystical.

Physically, ecstasy manifests itself as a trance. The trance may be short-lived or prolonged. During a trance, flashes of lucidity flood one's consciousness. Outwardly, a trance may take a violent form or even slide into "catalepsy." It carries "no guarantee of

---

24. Ibid., 81.
25. Ibid.
26. Ibid., 358.
27. Ibid.

spiritual value . . . [as it] merely indicates the presence of certain abnormal psycho-physical conditions."[28] For a religious mystic, however, an ecstatic trance is a vivid, real, and intimate consciousness of God.

Psychologically, ecstasy "is a form . . . of complete mono-ideism," a deliberate focus on *one thing* only. As such, it is "an exalted form of contemplation, . . . an exercise of the will . . . [a] contemplation carried to its highest pitch." Ecstasy is a withdrawal from all reception of the external world. It is the prelude for any unification of consciousness of the One. "The tide of life is withdrawn."[29] It can be triggered by any event, but for Christian mystics, "the sacraments and mysteries of faith have always provided its *point d'appui* [grounds of support]." It can result in feelings of levitation or even the sense of an "out-of-body" experience that floods the heart with peace and love.

Mystically, ecstasy is nothing short of "an exalted act of perception." One moves into the super-sensual world "in which . . . consciousness escapes the limitations of the senses, rises to freedom, and is united for an instant with the 'great life of the All.'"[30]

As for rapture, Underhill views it as "a violent and uncontrollable expression of genius for the Absolute," yielding results of splendor that validate life. Rapture is an "extra," not always part of an ecstatic or entrancement experience itself. It cannot be sought but is rather a given. This is what Pascal experienced, inspiring his own utterance of mystical sublimity: "Certitude, Peace, Joy!"[31] From the moment it occurs, rapture shapes the mystic's life. For Underhill, citing Richard of Saint Victor's words, it becomes "not a thirst *for* God but *into* God."[32]

How much of this applies to Paul is debatable. As a mystic, even viewed with a lowercase "m," his experiences of 2 Corinthians mirror everything Underhill suggests. Chapter 12 of 2 Corinthians

28. Ibid., 360.
29. Ibid., 364.
30. Ibid., 367.
31. Ibid., 376.
32. Ibid., 378.

5. Spiritual Consciousness: Its Depths and Dimensions

captures one after another of Underhill's points. Specifically, (1) *entrancement*, (2) *psychological unity with the highest form of reality*, (3) *levitation*, (4) and *mystical rapture* unite in Paul's description of one of the most intense spiritual moments contained in his letters. That it shaped Paul's life forever, becoming a moment he could never forget, as well as a "unification" he longed to experience, is clearly apparent. As we have noted before, it deserves repeating:

> It is necessary to boast; nothing is to be gained by it, but I will go on to visions and revelations of the Lord. I know a person in Christ who fourteen years ago was caught up to the third heaven—whether in the body or out of the body I do not know; God knows. And I know that such a person—whether in the body or out of the body I do not know: God knows—was caught up into Paradise and heard things that are not to be told, that no mortal is permitted to repeat. (2 Cor 12:1–4)

No other passage communicates Paul's mysticism with greater forcefulness. Paul witnesses to the full power of such moments to lift one into the very realm of the All, blocking out all consciousness of the things below such that one might be absorbed into the Divine Consciousness of the All in all. There is no shame in scholarship acknowledging this, nor is there any need to deny its occurrence or spiritual power in Paul's life.

Of course, Underhill's study is "full of high-sentence and a bit obtuse," to borrow T. S. Eliot's assessment of Prufrock's silent interiority. Nevertheless, Underhill's work addresses the essence of every quest for full self-attainment and self-identity vis-à-vis the Reality of Being in the midst of one's own journey of becoming.

By way of summation, perhaps we can argue that there exist four types of mysticism or spiritual consciousness that tug for attention in one form or other. Within reason, they may be identified as metaphysical, spiritual, ecstatic, and vital.

Metaphysical mysticism emerges as a conscious awareness of the transcendental, or of that which defines life and constitutes the ground of one's being. In its theological or more philosophical form, metaphysical mysticism borders on the recognition that one's existentiality is inseparable from the highest reality of life one can conceive, being mirrored in the Old Testament's concept of the *imago dei*, or that humanity's essence is a manifestation of the mystery of God.

Metaphysical mysticism is both cognitive and intellectual. It is rooted in one's deep hunger to understand oneself, reality, and the meaning of existence. To that extent, it is Platonic and rational, favoring idealism over materialism, thought over substance, Being over becoming, and the Eternal over time—yet never at the expense of the Universal drowning out the personality of the individual, and always itself honoring what is good, beautiful, and true.

Spiritual mysticism is more holistic, profoundly individual, heart-to-heart, intuitive, at times inexpressible and incommunicable but never haughty or irrational. It longs for the order of innocence and purity, to hear the voice of God in one's silence as well as in one's searching, joy, and sorrow. It knows how to be abased and how to abound, how to give and how to receive, how to suffer and how to conquer, how to live and how to die.

We see spiritual mysticism in the lives of Abraham, Sarah, Moses, and Ruth. It comes to us full-force in the mystery of Jesus as well as in the life of the Buddha. It speaks to us in the lives and letters of saints like Augustine, Saint Francis, Theresa, Meister Eckhart, the Dalai Lama, and others, as well in as Saint Paul. On its wings it brings healing and mercy, mending and catharsis, renewal and inspiration, humility and the grace to care about others. It touches our hearts in Paul's letters and, with power and insight, appeals to us to join him in his mystic union with the Christ of faith, whose historical existence manifests the very soul of God.

Ecstatic mysticism is entirely other. It lifts one into the realm of the truly Ineffable—the Transcendent beyond words. It eludes every symbolic representation. Like fire, it consumes self-consciousness, bearing the soul into an all-embracing light and bliss, as Paul himself described for the Corinthians. It stands as the supreme encounter with the Holiest Holy, the Perfect and Eternal Reality beyond all fetters that time represents. It is the "That Thou

5. Spiritual Consciousness: Its Depths and Dimensions

Art" of Eastern mysticism, the "I am that I am" of Hebrew Scriptures, and the Logos Divine of John's Gospel.

As for vital mysticism, it constitutes one's natural feelings of union with nature or the universe itself. It can be animistic or neutral, as represented in the spiritual elements of Shinto or the Mystic Way of Taoism. We encounter it as well in process philosophy and in the latter's awareness of our ontological unity with the forces of the evolving universe in all its quantum wonder and star-flung glory, or as simple and fulfilling as a hiker's trek through a flowering meadow or restful walk under the graceful boughs of soughing pines beside a crystal brook.

Where do we each come down? What form of mysticism best fulfills our own secret depths? Paul urged his followers to choose "an in-Christ mysticism," wherein the glory of God came down in human form as a historical given and not merely as an ideal. How we each come out is no simple choice to make. "For now, we see in a glass dimly," said Paul. "But how we should love to know God face-to-face!"

For that reason, our chapter nudges us to end on a cautionary note that theologians request us to consider. We acknowledged it in chapter 1 under "Pillar Two." If the Transcendent has not, or cannot, initiate or address our human restlessness, and if the Eternal cannot stir our souls in the form of wonder—as in the case of Moses and the burning bush or Elijah upon hearing the still, small voice—then may not our experiences of the Ineffable amount to little more than subjective reflections and longings of the human condition, thus diminishing any sense of the presence of God or the trans-phenomenal, much less any resulting "epiphany" with the divine? Paul understood as much, which perhaps explains why he advised the Corinthians that he resolved to know Christ only, "and him crucified" (1 Cor 2:2). Yet even having said this, transcendence and meditation, in their self-emptying form, remain nonetheless a "silence before God."

6. Pillar Three: The Righteousness of God

"The righteousness of God" (*dikaiosuné theou*) is Paul's answer to the age-old question to which we have referred all along. It appears in the psalmist's plea: "What are human beings that you are mindful of them?" (Ps 8:4). Indeed, what would befall humankind if God were not mindful of human life? What if there were no higher realm of transcendence than the self to bear one's hopes and fate? For Paul, the power of the gospel speaks to this very condition: that it is God who makes whole what humanity cannot, a task that only God can do. Indeed, the making of humankind "whole" is what "the righteousness of God" achieves.

We have seen how Heidegger addressed the issue in the form of his concept of "dread," which plunges one into the pit of "Nothingness" in search of the answer, as well as in Tillich's analysis of humankind's ontological condition in terms of its tripartite fears: the fear of Non-being, the anxiety of existential doubt, and the fear of meaninglessness.[1] The righteousness of God addresses all three and resolves Heidegger's "dread" as well. It does so by offering humankind redemption from forfeiture and inauthenticity, along with inner renewal and inner peace.

In an equally philosophical sense, it answers Sartre's search for the meaning of "being-for-itself" as well as Camus' resigned acceptance of the "absurdity" of life. Their starting point was Nietzsche's "Death of God," but that does not have to be one's ontological or spiritual launching pad. In truth, every starting point is a leap into the void, the very position Heidegger was trying to establish,

---

1. Tillich, *Systematic Theology*, 186–203.

6. Pillar Three: The Righteousness of God

which constitutes an encounter with that which transcends the self. That Sartre and Camus elected to reject any transcendence higher than the inner self is hardly a rejection of transcendence; rather, it represents an epistemological "starting point" based on the denial of traditional metaphysics and theism. Their search for a foundation from which to initiate their own definition of what makes one "whole" or "right" or "fulfilled" nonetheless remains an act of transcendence.

Both philosophers above recognized as much, yet they were adamant concerning the risk. In the end, both found that to justify their own position they had to embrace "others" (i.e., transcend themselves), inasmuch as what they assumed to be their right philosophically could not be denied to others. If I have the right to define myself, then I have to extend that same right to you, which is ipso facto an act of transcendence, once again.

We cannot help but put ourselves to the question, cognizant that we are mindful of ourselves, a fact that Sartre fully acknowledges. But to avoid having to answer the question in any form of past metaphysical positions, Sartre chose to eliminate the concept of a "human essence," or of a person with an entity having a nature, or as a being dependent on any quasi-ontological grounds that would require any human to attain a goal not set by the self. Human beings have no purpose they have to fulfill. Such a notion of being a "being" with an end to pursue is purposeless. If we have any "facticity," Sartre concludes, then it lies in the fact "that I am condemned to be wholly responsible for myself. I am the being which is in such a way that in its being its being is in question."[2] Even so, this leads to anguish and a sense of abandonment, of "being thrown into the world" without one's consent. Furthermore, it results in the realization that one has to "decide the meaning of being" for oneself. One cannot escape this responsibility, but on the positive side, it means one is free to determine one's own path, to set the course of one's own history, however one chooses. States Sartre:

---

2. Sartre, *Being and Nothingness*, 494.

Transcendence and Fulfilment

> The one who realizes in anguish his condition as being thrown into a responsibility which extends to his very abandonment has no longer either remorse or regret or excuse; he is no longer anything but a freedom which perfectly reveals itself and whose being resides in this very revelation.[3]

Though he denies that there is any such reality as a human essence or a human nature, Sartre was willing to acknowledge the existence of "a universal human condition." That we are born into a time, a world, an economic and social period all its own is a fact of life. We might not have been able to choose the time, the era, the period, or our social, economic, or class situation. They are given. But what remains true is that to exist in such a world, we have "to be at work there, to be there in the midst of other people, and to be mortal there."[4] Again, however, this "universality of man" is not an ironclad given. States Sartre: "It is perpetually being made. I build the universal in choosing myself; I build it in understanding the configuration of every other man," who must do the same.[5]

We shall come back to this, but however atheistic or rigid Sartre's position may appear, the phenomenon of transcendence is present in his work at every level. What are we that we feel impelled to project God as life's highest answer and not ourselves? Why does the anguish burn until humankind does, or even in its rejection of God, continue to seek a solution to its mystery? And what of Sartre's "starting point," that we "are thrown into the world"? No one is "thrown into the world." Human beings are born of parents and, at least in most of the world, were and are wanted and are loved and supported until able to live on their own. Transcendence is not Sartre's sole property. Even Aristotle argued that there is a formal and final cause behind human existence that far outweighs its material and agent causes. Biological creatures we are, but we are also gifted with curiosity— a hunger and desire to know—and with a self-consciousness that can bear one's spirit into

---

3. Ibid., 495.
4. Ibid., *Existentialism*, 528.
5. Ibid., 529.

6. Pillar Three: The Righteousness of God

the inner depths or upward into the highest spheres of knowledge and wonder. And this it does until it feels at one with the origins of Being and at peace with the All in all. Tillich referred to the latter as the "Ground of Being," a putative reality as inescapable from our creature-hood as breathing and hope.

In his time and place, Paul too was faced with life's ironies and dilemmas and found in the righteousness of God the secret to existence. For Paul, it contained the *euangelion* that for all that burdens and strikes humanity down, God—the Highest Order of the Eternal—bears humanity up into his holy goodness and loving righteousness. There, in the bonds of God's self-giving love made manifest in the death and resurrection of the Christ, one finds purpose again. One finds forgiveness and redemption, strength and consolation, beyond every threat of Non-being, feeling of dread, remorse, or abandonment, or encounter with Death and Nothingness. We were meant to live and have life abundantly—whether in its most Platonic form or humanistic pursuit. For Paul, that is why the righteousness of God constitutes the power of salvation.

Paul's language, along with his cultural, mystical, and religious worldview, may seem quaint and foreign to us now, but the underlying truth of his insight is not. That redemption is necessary to wipe away every impediment that enslaves a life, forcing it to be less than whole, is as psychologically relevant today as it was in Paul's time. Since the time of Freud, Jung, and Adler, the necessity of bringing to light the dread and darkness of human forfeiture, of its "fallenness" and "inauthenticity," has been commonly recognized among most theories and therapies of counseling. It is hardly accidental, therefore, that one's immersion in such therapies can lead to the alleviation of guilt as well as to victory over abandonment and remorse, despair, or shame, resulting in renewal and hope.

"Out of the depths I cry to you, O Lord," is the way the psalmist put it, adding, "If you, O Lord, should mark iniquities, who could stand? But there is forgiveness with you, so that you may be revered" (Ps 130:1, 4). In Paul's case, it is the Christ who makes possible this righteousness: "For while we were still weak, at the right time Christ died for the ungodly . . . But God proves his love for us in that while we still were sinners Christ died for us" (Rom 5:6–8). That is the essence of the Order of the Spirit that redeems and elucidates existence, satisfying one's ontological quest with wholeness and peace.

By further analysis, one may appeal equally to Gabriel Marcel and his neo-Socratic program. Without taking Marcel out of context, he offered a redemptive assessment of his own with respect to "mystery and being." States Marcel: "the Mysterious and Ontological are identical."[6] Marcel was a contemporary of Sartre's, as every bit as much a Frenchman and heir to European theism as was Sartre. Yet he concluded that the mystery of Being, or "ontological mystery," is so embedded in the human predicament as to be unavoidable in terms of addressing the essence of existence. Marcel argues that there is a critical difference between what we call "the Problematic" and "the Mysterious." The "Problematic" can be identified and solved as something outside ourselves, as it does not require our participation and ontological bearing. But not so "the Mysterious," which was Marcel's choice term for the Transcendent, for it "is something in which I find myself caught up, and whose essence is therefore not to be before me in its entirety. It is as though in this province the distinction between *in me* and *before* me loses its meaning."[7] In other words, it is the awareness of this mystery that opens the possibility to discovering one's ontological wholeness. As with Paul, this too is an act of faith. Marcel elaborates: "a mystery is something in which I am myself involved, and it can therefore only be thought of as a sphere where the distinction between what is in me and what is before me loses its meaning and its initial validity."[8] In this sphere, one acts in all things on an intuition one possesses without realizing one possesses it. One awakens to the realization that one is "not simply identical with his own life" but with something far greater. Marcel considered this a form of "fearless critical reflection." It can lead

6. Marcel, *Being and Having*, 617.
7. Ibid.
8. Ibid., 621.

6. Pillar Three: The Righteousness of God

to despair, even suicide, but on deeper examination exposes the choices of despair or suicide as acts of "betrayal" or "overpassing" (*Aufhebung*) similar to Heidegger's "forfeiture." Hence, any "concrete approaches to the ontological mystery should not be sought in the scale of logical thought, . . . [but] in the elucidation of certain data which are spiritual in their own right, such [as] fidelity, hope and love, where we may see man at grips with the temptations of denial, introversion, and hard-heartedness."[9] Of these three (fidelity, hope, and love), fidelity matters most at the ontological level, as it signals "an ontological permanency" that, in Marcel's mind, only God can guarantee. Thus, against all temptations to settle for a Kantian or Sartrean "autocentricity," Marcel pleads for a lifelong openness "to the presence of mystery, which is the foundation of [everyone's] very being, and apart from which [there is] nothingness." Indeed, the whole sphere of religion, art, and metaphysics find its home in this mystery.[10]

Marcel's interpretation may be closer to Paul's than anyone else's. This is especially the case concerning the human condition and its need to experience an ontological restoration from the fear of nothingness. It is this fear that is clearly addressed and resolved in the apostle's principle of the "righteousness of God," which alone guarantees humankind's joy and peace in the face of angst and the dread of Nothingness.

A closer look at Paul's references to God's righteousness in his own words, however, is requisite. Schweitzer detected no less than two Pauline doctrines concerning the atoning death of Christ. One involves "the forgiveness of sins" through the concept of "righteousness of faith," while the other was developed "as a whole from the mystical doctrine of being-in-Christ."[11] Schweitzer considered the latter of far more importance, as it provided the insight that made it possible for Paul to break with the Law, inasmuch as one's "dying in Christ" freed one from the curse of the Law. Simply being "forgiven" did not require the nullification of the Law. One

9. Ibid., 622.
10. Ibid., 628.
11. Schweitzer, *Mysticism of Paul*, 221.

could have still lived under the Law. Something else had to occur to liberate one from its dominance.

Scripturally, the doctrine of the forgiveness of sins through the righteousness of faith abounds throughout Paul's Epistle to the Romans. Most notable is Rom 3:21–26:

> But now, apart from the law, the righteousness of God has been disclosed, and is attested by the law and the prophets, the righteousness of God through faith in Jesus Christ for all who believe. For there is no distinction, since all have sinned and fall short of the glory of God; they are now justified by his grace as a gift, through the redemption that is in Christ Jesus, whom God put forward as a sacrifice of atonement by his blood, effective through faith. He did this to show his righteousness, because in his divine forbearance he has passed over the sins previously committed; it was to prove at the present time that he himself is righteous and that he justifies the one who has faith in Jesus. (Rom 3:21–26)

In this passage, Paul presents Christ as having fulfilled the "sin offerings" required of Lev 4:22–6:7 and Lev 16:1–27. In Christ's atoning death, all past sin is now forgiven. Paul reiterates this theme again in Rom 5:1–2: "Therefore, since we are justified by faith, we have peace with God through our Lord Jesus Christ, through whom we have obtained access to this grace in which we stand."

Schweitzer found the above intriguing, as it in no way required the negation of the Law. Something else was stirring in Paul, drawn from his mystical in-Christ unification. Schweitzer dubs Paul's doctrine of the atonement form of righteousness an "intellectual" doctrine, drawn primarily from reflection. Unfortunately, it became the central doctrine of the later church and especially of the Reformation. In its favor, this doctrine promoted redemption as "individualistic and uncosmic," a redemption "that takes place between God, Christ, and the believer."[12]

---

12. Ibid., 219.

6. Pillar Three: The Righteousness of God

Paul, however, was in tune with a second insight, driven by his "in-Christ mysticism," with its complete freedom from the Law. Schweitzer labels it a "quasi-physical" concept of redemption, more powerful than its "intellectual" twin. This quasi-physical redemption of Paul's mysticism is "a collective, cosmically-conditioned event" and the insight that made it possible for Paul to claim that he has been crucified with Christ, so that the life he now lives he lives in Christ Jesus. This claim—combined with Paul's concept of Adam as the "first man," or a natural (psychic) man belonging to the created order, and of Christ as the "second Adam" (a spiritual or pneumatic man) descended from heaven—launched a cosmic event effective for all who have died in Christ (1 Cor 15:22, 45–49). Hence, Paul can state that "as many of you as were baptized into Christ have clothed yourselves with Christ . . . there is no longer Jew or Greek, there is no longer slave or free, there is no longer male and female, for all of you are one in Christ Jesus" (Gal 3:27–28). For Schweitzer, this constituted Paul's true, favored doctrine of atonement, as its strength lies in uniting humanity with God, resulting in a new creation of ontological completeness and liberation to live for Christ, free of the bonds of the Law that the fallen angels had turned into a curse.[13]

Paul's dual doctrine is remarkable and deserves to be accepted as such. Though its ancient language and assumptions and Greco-Hebraic undertones may no longer conform to our own, Paul's vision of wholeness and redemption, made possible through the Highest Transcendence become flesh, has the power to awaken humanity's hunger to be whole in itself. To that extent, the views of Heidegger, Sartre, Camus, Tillich, and Marcel represent methodologies in search of wholeness that one can explore for oneself.

Upon deeper reflection, the answer to the human condition depends on one's definition of that condition. Tillich's tripartite fears of Non-being, existential doubt, and meaninglessness provide only one set of conditions that human wholeness must address. So is it too in the case of Paul's understanding of humankind's

---

13. Ibid., 213–14.

inability to rise above its sin, doubt, and disobedience without God's forgiving grace.

Augustine's own analysis of the human condition equally addressed humanity's anthropological situation and did so for centuries: that Adam's pride led ultimately to ignorance, concupiscence, and finally death. To this he added his neoplatonic interpretation of the City of God, a reality whose transcendent values of faith, hope, and love saves humankind from the foibles of the City of Man. As with the individual, society is also beset by avarice and greed, lust and power, cruelty and pain. That is why the human heart will forever remain restless until it rests in God.

In summation, perhaps the following might be offered regarding the human situation:

1. We are a puzzle unto ourselves, often as uncertain as to what to believe as incapable of discovering it. This paradoxical irony extends to one's place and time in the universe as well as to any ontological self-awareness a person may possess. It is intensely personal and problematic—so much so that one often fails to transcend one's own interiority or ability to appreciate the plight and misgivings of others. To say that one is alienated from oneself, others, or the Eternal is to put it mildly. If alienation counts at all, the self rarely views itself as the "alienating one." Rather, one sees oneself as the victim of this state of alienation, dread, or encounter with Nothingness, not its progenitor. Within that context, exploration of the necessity of relating to the self, to others, and to the Eternal bears healing merit.

2. That we experience remorse is an inescapable factor of existence. Most human beings at some point come to regret their impulsive, angry, or cruel treatment of others, whatever prompted their actions. Knowing that such behavior can never be reversed—that one cannot roll back time to undo hurt inflicted on others—creates the "sickness unto death" whose consequence Kierkegaard explored in depth. Only forgiveness (i.e., the willingness to forgive on both the part

6. Pillar Three: The Righteousness of God

of the offender and the offended) ultimately awakens one's determination to change attitudes and behavior for the better.

3. So too does the sense of one's mortality take center stage. The sands of one's hourglass are ever slipping away.

   > O LORD, God of my salvation, . . . let my prayer come before you; . . . For my soul is full of troubles, and my life draws near to Sheol. I am counted among those who go down to the Pit; . . . like those forsaken among the dead, like the slain that lie in the grave, like those whom you remember no more. (Ps 88:1–5)

   It is this "remembrance no more" that tears at the human soul, that devours our sense of belonging to the Eternal, and that, if ever lost, undoes our unique personality and sense of worth as individuals.

   We find it addressed again in Ps 89: "How long, O LORD? Will you hide yourself forever? Remember how short my time is—for what vanity you have created all mortals! Who can live and never see death? Who can escape the power of Sheol?" (vv. 46–48). In the psalmist's mind, if it were not for God's steadfast love and faithfulness to the house of David, hope would be nonexistent.

4. Because transcendence provides that hope, or in Marcel's words, the Mystery of mysteries invites us to explore life's depths, we are enabled to shoulder the irony of existence and to do so with courage. Imprisoned in each human vessel, a will to live surfaces to shape one's sensibilities and need to act. Religion maintains that God ordained it so, creating humankind in God's own "image" to rule and strive in order to make God's world a mirror of God's goodness. Slave as well as master of our biological and physiological existence, our interiority presses us forward to engage in the world and write our history as best we can. Bristling against the angst of death, we overcome death itself in the courageous way we live.

5. For the above to become a reality, one must reach deep into one's inner being to find the will and faith to make it so. Only the self can do this for itself. No one can believe for anyone

but oneself, though as a leitmotif running throughout Scripture, God's unconquerable will and Spirit are ever at work wooing the soul to say, "Yes!" Therein lies the secret of God's Deity and the prayer that one is "elect."

6. To that extent, the human soul needs another—a guide, a friend, a mentor, a companion like none other. That is what Christ became for Paul, or in the case of the young prince Arjuna, what Vishnu became when he descended in the form of Krishna to guide the youth into the battle of life. Such visions of transcendence are never to be disparaged.

That is why *transcendence* in the form of the *historical*—become visible and knowable in the Christ of Nazareth, or in Plato's writings *incarnate* in the life of Socrates—becomes the wellspring of fulfillment and the guarantor of one's existence. Metaphorically as well as metaphysically, it is God's transcendent goodness, shining brightly on the holy mountain of life's mystery, that guides one ultimately to its summit of peace and wholeness. Nonetheless, only to the extent that God's divine life, will, grace, and self-emptying are appropriated into our personal lives do we change and discover that the divine call hardly rests in us alone; inevitably, it summons us *to love others* as we love ourselves. It simply cannot stop with the self and be of God. That is every religion's highest truth in answer to the human condition.

Before concluding this chapter, one further exploration of the anthropological problem is worth reviewing: that conducted by Nicolas Berdyaev. His Russian Orthodox views cut straight into the heart of the discussion and offer incalculable insight.

As Berdyaev ventures: "Man is a profound riddle to himself, for he bears witness to the existence of a higher world." Our disconnection with ourselves is a constituent element of the human condition and leads humanity to realize that we belong to two worlds: one natural, the other supernatural. Thus, we embody a "self-contradictory" as well as a "paradoxical" element—one reflective of our fallen nature, the other "preserving memories of

6. Pillar Three: The Righteousness of God

heaven," inasmuch as we are children of God with roots in heaven, not just in nature.[14]

The three major branches of Christianity have viewed this condition differently. In Berdyaev's mind, Catholicism views man as a natural being whose fall can only be restored by the supernatural graces of faith, hope, and love. Through the fall, humans lost the latter, but through Christ's death and resurrection, these virtues can be regained. But, claims Berdyaev, "man . . . as a natural being suffered comparatively little damage." This view errs, therefore, insofar as it does injustice "to the Divine image and likeness in man and may lead to a purely naturalistic interpretation of human nature." As for the Protestant conception, the fall "completely ruined and distorted human nature, clouding man's reasoning, depriving him of freedom, and reducing him to live up to what God has created him to be. From such a point of view human nature can never be hallowed and transfigured" again.[15] As for Berdyaev's own Russian Orthodox view, it hallows the "doctrine of the Divine image and likeness in man—the doctrine i.e. that man has been created as a spiritual being." The fall never destroyed this image; rather, the fall "damaged" it. Through divine grace and love, one's spiritual being can flower again and thus attain wholeness for oneself and society.[16]

Whatever may be said of Christianity, at least for Berdyaev, it "faces the problem of man and clearly sees what a paradoxical being man is." Christianity thus recognizes our tragic side as well as our potential to do good and, in this respect, is superior to all other theories regarding the human condition.[17] Christianity further acknowledges the conflict between equal values that tug on humankind's heart every day. By preserving the doctrine of the divine image and humankind's spiritual nature, Christianity views

---

14. Berdyaev, *Destiny of Man*, 60.
15. Ibid., 61.
16. Ibid.
17. Ibid., 62.

humanity as a being who "humanizes nature" and in doing so, "humanizes the idea of God, and through this humanizes himself."[18]

Furthermore, this dual nature of humanity accounts for humankind's "primeval, utterly undetermined potential freedom springing from the abyss of non-being, and the element determined by the fact that man is the image and likeness of God."[19] God's will is communicated to the world and enacted through human activity. Because of humanity's dual nature, we will always long to hear the voice of God, but we can only hear it in and through ourselves. We are our own mediators between the divine and our natural world. In this way, God is able to "express Himself" through interaction with humankind, "through meeting man, through man's answering His call, through the refraction of the divine principle in human freedom. Hence the extraordinary complexity of the religious life."[20]

Far more could be said of Berdyaev's analysis, but we shall return to it again in chapter 10, where Berdyaev focuses exclusively on humanity's fate and destiny as lived vis-à-vis the Eternal.

---

18. Ibid.
19. Ibid., 70.
20. Ibid.

7. Pillar Four: Apollonian Restraint in a Dionysian Age

It may seem strange to commence a chapter on Paul's fourth pillar of wisdom by setting it in perspective with the Greek gods Apollo and Dionysus, but there is a justifiable reason for doing so. Apollo was the offspring of Zeus and Leto; Dionysus was born of Zeus and Semele. Their significance to the Greek world dominated and inspired lives for many years. Their direct worship may have waned by the time of Paul, but not their symbolic importance.

The mythological lore associated with each Greek god has been published and explored by numerous scholars, especially by Germany's Walter Burkert in his *Greek Religion* and by American grand dame Edith Hamilton in her notable work *Mythology: Timeless Tales of Gods and Heroes*. Both Apollo and Dionysus are important because they represent opposing views of wholeness. In Nietzsche's mind, they were essential to the birth of the Greek tragedies as Athenians strove to wrestle with the meaning of their culture.

In time, Apollo, the young god of perfect manhood, became the champion and upholder of tragic justice. This movement came about as the youthful hunter matured to realize that "murder demands atonement," yet that even "catastrophe" can be "overcome . . . through expiation" and suffering. As Burkert continues:

> In mythology Apollo himself is made subject to this law; after slaying the Cyclopes he is banished from Olympus, and after killing the Python he is obliged to leave Delphi and seek purification in the distant Temple valley in

Transcendence and Fulfilment

Thessaly. Following Aeschylus, it was also imagined that he had personally carried out the bloody purification of Orestes in the temple at Delphi. In the last book of the *Iliad*, when Achilles ... continues to violate Hector's corpse, Apollo protests as the advocate of purity: 'He disfigures the dumb earth in his fury,' ... Man is able to make an end with things and to start afresh in awareness of his own limits.[1]

As time passed, Delphi became known for its famous inscriptions, one of which Socrates would quote and take as his principal norm: "know thyself" (*gnothi sauton*). A second equally famous inscription read, "nothing in excess" (*meden agan*).[2] Both imperatives were attributed to Apollo and became mainstays in Greek philosophical thought from Plato's time onward. Paul might not have known of either dictum, though that is hardly unlikely, but his system of ethics certainly appropriates their truth. They were part of the fabric of the era.

As the god of the vine, Dionysus became the symbol of exuberance and the ecstatic state of intoxication, coupled with the uncontrollable madness, fury, and destructive behavior of his followers. He would become associated with immortality and the gift of afterlife. Together, the two gods attracted both the philosophical as well as the antinomian sentiments of the time.

In our modern era, it was Nietzsche who wed the two insights together, claiming that the two themes (restraint and exuberance) marked a breakthrough in Greek thought, leading to a tragic sense of life that would be mirrored in the tragedies of Greece's playwrights. Nonetheless, for Nietzsche, neither the ancient world nor his contemporary era needed to choose between the two, since a whole person requires a balance of these twin themes in order to achieve equilibrium. One cannot simply deny the "flesh" and exalt the "spirit" or reverse the two and experience a complete existence. Where exuberance is suppressed or despised, society becomes susceptible to "priests" and their doctrines of "resentment," hypocrisy,

1. Burkert, *Greek Religion*, 148.
2. Ibid.

7. Pillar Four: Apollonian Restraint in a Dionysian Age

and envy. A Dionysian creativity is essential to fulfillment. At the same time, however, restraint is equally necessary. Nietzsche expounded as much in the form of an "Apollonian will" determined to "overcome" the worst in oneself and society, thus nudging Nietzsche to create his concept of the *Ubermensch*, or "Overman," who balances the appetitive and rational dimensions of humanity's dual nature.[3]

In part, Nietzsche was drawing upon Plato's imagery of the self in *Phaedrus* and elsewhere, where "reason" is depicted as a charioteer, standing in his chariot's rickety frame, guiding his two steeds of "appetite" and "will" toward the high calling of the "Good." Only where appetite is kept in check by the will, which in turn is kept in check by reason's submission to wisdom, can the charioteer hope to reach his goal. Otherwise, the weight of his chariot, led off-course by appetite, will waver and plunge back to earth in a disheartening *katabolé*, or tragic fall. Plato's depiction of the struggle between appetite and will, or flesh and spirit, has never lost its illuminating power. Paul seizes upon its universality in his own assessment of "the works of the flesh" versus the "life of the Spirit." One cannot be a whole person if one's soul is captive to the perverse will of the "flesh." One must restrain it if one's life in Christ is to mean anything at all.

If we turn to Philippians by way of a preamble, we find that Phil 2:15 captures something of the daunting challenge Paul faced in addressing the moral situation of his new converts. Their Greco-Asian world of values could no longer suffice as a basis for a life in Christ. Whatever their social or economic status, their hearts needed to be guided by a wisdom and spirit heretofore untapped. Otherwise, they would be unable to cope "in the midst of a crooked and perverse generation" (*méson geneas skolias kai diestramménas*) in which Paul wanted them to shine like stars to the glory to God.

We are familiar with the Greek word *skolias*, as it has since become part of our medical lore as "scoliosis," a devastating disease that leaves one's spinal column bent and twisted, affecting one's life

---

3. Nietzsche, *Gay Science*, 283.

from head to toe. In Greek thought and language, it was a moral disorder as well. Paul did not want its debilitating effects to disable his Philippians' hearts. The second noun is equally intriguing: *diestramménas*. It is derived from the verb *diastrépho*, meaning "to pervert, corrupt, or cause a defect"—a Greek concept that long predated Paul. Aristotle made "defect" a central factor in creating his own list of restraining Apollonian tenets. Likewise, for Paul, one cannot indulge in the perverse world of one's Gentile state and be a shining sphere of good for others, let alone for God. Paul fully acknowledged the impossibility of ceasing to live in the world (1 Cor 6:9–10). Nothing is gained by withdrawing from it. Nor did he feel justified in judging those who did, but if one is a new creation in Christ—a discoverer of God's longed-for ontological wholeness of existence—then one should want to change one's life out of gratitude for God's love. It is to that effect that Paul admonished his Corinthian converts: "Do you not realize that Jesus Christ is in you?" (2 Cor 13:5).

Just how "perverse" his converts' generation was is reiterated throughout Paul's letters. Paul provides "documented" lists of its perversities along with its vices, which in his Corinthian letters he reminds his readers they once *practiced*.

If we turn to Romans first, however, we discover Paul's list of humankind's perverse shortcomings *in general*. His point is that all humankind is burdened by these faults. The list is formidable. It contains "the lust of the heart, degrading passions, cohabitation with members of the same sex, [possessors of] debased minds, [practicing] wickedness, evil, covetousness, malice, envy, murder, strife, deceit, craftiness, [becoming thereby] gossips, slanderers, God-haters, insolent, haughty, boastful, inventors of evil, rebellious toward parents, foolish, faithless, heartless, and ruthless" (Rom 1:24–32), rendering them guilty of "impertinent hearts, self-seeking" (2:5, 8) and given to "stealing, adultery, and idolatry" (2:22) as well as "reveling in drunkenness, debauchery, and jealousy" (13:13). In Paul's mind, these vices provide an extensive catalog descriptive of the human condition in everyone's present state of "forfeiture" or "inauthenticity." Therefore, one's failure to

7. Pillar Four: Apollonian Restraint in a Dionysian Age

understand one's condition compromises one's capacity to fathom Apollo's searching dictum—*know thyself*—essential if one is to change and become whole. In Paul's case, it took the injunctions of the Law to wake him up, while at the same time steeping him in guilt.

If one studies Paul's Romans list carefully, a reader will note that his "defects" fall into two categories: one detailing *the marks of human frailty* according to the "flesh," the other exposing humanity's *interior depths of fear and discord*, or one's inner spirit. We have already addressed Paul's acknowledged *sarcophobia*, or disdain for the things below, but in the end any equilibrium of soul and body, heart and flesh, still falls beyond one's capacity to reconcile. This leads to the apostle's own acknowledgment that though he longed to do what was right, Paul found himself unable to accede to his will, thus breaking the coveted link that he so wanted to preserve between the Infinite God of love and his own finite particularity. Only Christ could save him now.

There is validity in this *gnothi sauton* dictum. It constitutes a major facet of the realization of one's soul in conflict with itself, with others, and with the Eternal. It explains why transcendence is paramount to Marcel's distinction between "having and being," as the pursuit of the material alone can never make a being whole. If our lives are to become richer, then for Marcel, we simply have to risk launching into what is beyond mere "having," for life is so much more than the satiation of one's erotic, materialistic, and covetous desires. In Marcel's judgment, we must welcome the invitation to participate in life's mystery in the hope of discovering the deeper Order of the Spirit. For Paul, the heart must simply say no to what it knows is base and demeaning if one's equilibrium is to experience God's fullest joy.

This is nothing new. Socrates had to question himself in order to grasp the Oracle's meaning of the "know thyself" dictum, as the latter taught him that inasmuch as he considered himself the least wise Athenian, he became the most wise and thus open to listening and searching for the highest Good. Paul found the same in opening his soul to the miracle of the Universal and Sole

God of his people, who, in dispatching his Son in the form of the historical Jesus of Nazareth, made it possible for him to experience a new heart and being. Ontology cannot be divorced from ethics or from how one lives.

This brings us back to Paul and his lists of Apollonian restraints. One cannot be free if one is bound to what limits the Order of the Spirit. "All things are lawful for me," Paul notes, "but not all things are beneficial." Or, as he continues, "All things are lawful," but "I will not be dominated by anything" (1 Cor 6:12).

Paul shares much in common with both his Jewish heritage and the philosophical mind-set of his era. As Victor Furnish reminds his readers, much of Paul's ethical thought was rooted in his people's self-understanding of God's having called them to be a holy nation, set apart from and unlike the godless cultures around them. That is what it meant to be "holy." Notes Furnish: "this most fundamental summons [based on the Holiness Code] is to *holiness*, and this summons, like holiness itself, has a theological basis: 'Speak to all the congregation of the people of Israel and say to them: "You shall be holy for I the LORD your God am holy"' (Lev 19:2).[4]

It is little wonder, then, that Paul finds the Greco-Roman world into which Christ has called him to preach mired in a sinking culture of moral rot—bent, twisted, and sadly culpable of its coming decay. Long before his indictment, Socrates bemoaned his own fellow Athenians' preference for wealth and power over the obvious priority of the care and improvement of the soul. Likewise, Aristotle in his *Nicomachean Ethics* developed a calculus of values to offset his era's proclivity to pursue wasteful *excess* on the one hand with its *defect* of character-eroding behavior on the other, instead of people fulfilling their highest potential: *the contemplation of reason above all*. It was this rational underpinning, or *logos*, that became flesh in Jesus' life and inspired Jesus to live in the light of God's kingdom now, which defined the gospel for John. It did for Paul as well, who incorporated it within his larger "in-Christ mysticism," which after his passing transformed the Christian movement of his day into a worldwide religion.

4. Furnish, *Moral Teaching*, 61.

7. Pillar Four: Apollonian Restraint in a Dionysian Age

When we turn to Paul's Corinthian correspondence, we find that Paul's earliest concerns were similar to the views he propounded in his Letter to the Romans. Here too, Paul's list of destabilizing choices captures the *excesses* and *defects* of a lifestyle no longer appropriate for a new being in Christ. His list focuses on a host of debilitating vices that distract the human will and erode the depths of one's inner self, leaving it in desperate need of forgiveness. To think that he might find the members of the Corinthian church still engaged in "quarreling, jealousy, anger, selfishness, slander, gossip, conceit, and disorder," along with "impurity, sexual immorality and licentiousness," would break his heart, Paul warns (1 Cor 5:9–12; 6:9–10; 2 Cor 12:20–21). To belong to God should inspire one to become an *imitator* of Christ, not a lost soul still torn between the excesses and defects of one's baser nature and resentful spirit. Paul fears that he may even find some of them still "fornicators, idolaters, adulterers, male prostitutes, sodomites, thieves, greedy, drunkards, revilers, and robbers," as indeed once they were, he notes (1 Cor 6:9–10). Now, however, as temples of the Holy Spirit, it is time to change.

We find Paul's same concerns expressed in his Letter to the Galatians. Here, Paul specifically contrasts the "works of the flesh" with the "fruit of the Spirit." The two are simply incompatible. We shall save the examination of the latter for chapter 8, but here, as in the case with his Letter to the Romans, his "works of the flesh" contain both the sins of human frailty and the sins of one's suppressed, darker spirit of conflict and fear. The former include, once again, "fornication, impurity, licentiousness, drunkenness, carousing, and the like" (Rom 5:19–20), whereas the sins of discord involve "idolatries, sorcery, enmities, strife, jealously, anger, quarrels, dissensions, factions, [and] envy" (5:19–21). Paul knew that the second category creates a greater sense of wrong, abuse, and self-destruction than one's *katabolé* into the sins of the flesh.

It is not our duty here to criticize Paul's attitude, his values, or how he sought to apply them to his Gentile converts. Victor Furnish's *The Moral Teaching of Paul* provides an incisive assessment of Paul's moral teachings in their context as well as an interpolation of their value today.[5] But society's issues in our time differ markedly from Paul's, both at the personal and global level. The key for Paul is that the appropriation of the *transforming grace of God* should remain central. Each person, however spiritual or secular, inevitably benefits from exploring what promotes or implodes one's life. The same applies to cultures and nations, especially in terms of their constitutions and legal rights as they cope with the present and anticipate the future. Such entities are wise to weigh what edifies a nation's soul versus what leads to its demise, loss of purpose, and misguided pursuit of justice, peace, and goodwill. Such a form of transcendence never loses it power. From Paul's perspective, when the foregoing is pursued within the context of a mystical union with Christ, then all who are so blessed by that mystery will "shine like stars" to the glory of God.

Within this context, Marcel's plea for humankind to reconsider transcendence provides a helpful bridge between Paul's ontological new being in Christ and our modern era in search of its soul. Having witnessed the horrors of both World Wars and the idealistic movements that preceded and dominated that period, Marcel flinched against the notion that humankind would once again become subject and slave to the "techniques of human degradation" that modern society so often pursues. Neither Communism's totalitarianism, nor Sartre's "atheistic existentialism" struck Marcel as capable of liberating the human spirit to experience its highest potential. Emphasizing the "historical situation" in which human beings find themselves here and now, Marcel urged a return to "transcendence" as humankind's best hope for personal and international wholeness. Communism's effort to suppress individual hopes in favor of the state, as well as atheistic existentialism's emphasis on the immanent self to determine one's own fate, constituted modern forms of bondage, which he refused to endorse. Both reduce mankind to "materialistic postulates." Thus Marcel explored the realm of transcendence anew, finding it so

---

5. Ibid. See Furnish's discussion of today's issues surrounding marriage and divorce, homoeroticism, feminist concerns, and global mandates (ibid., 28–159).

7. Pillar Four: Apollonian Restraint in a Dionysian Age

appealing in Socrates' work as to refer to himself as a "Neo-Socratic." "The very essence," he writes, "of [such] modern techniques of degradation . . . consists precisely in putting the individual into a situation in which he loses touch with himself."[6] Such a "materialistic conception of the universe is radically incompatible with the idea of a free [person]."[7] He thus proposed humanity's best "recourse" was to turn to the "transcendent," which he defined as:

> a level of being, an order of the spirit, which is also the level and an order of grace, of mercy, of charity; and to proclaim . . . that we repudiate *in advance* the deeds and the acts that may be obtained from us by any sort of constraint [imposed by the materialistic isms of atheism or totalitarian states] whatsoever. We solemnly affirm, by the appeal to the transcendent, that the reality of our selves lies *beyond* any such acts and any such words . . . What we have to do is to proclaim that we do *not* belong entirely to the world of objects to which men are seeking to assimilate us, in which they are straining to imprison us. . . . [Thus] a man cannot be free or remain free, except in the degree to which he remains linked with that which transcends him.[8]

Paul's ethic is clearly in accord with Marcel's interpolation of the power of transcendence and its capacity to shape human life. Assessing it in that light can be most beneficial.

A look at one of Paul's most distinguished contemporaries, however, is equally illuminating, inasmuch as the Stoic Lucius Annaeus Seneca shared many of Paul's moral views. It is doubtful that Paul knew of him, insofar as Seneca's fame did not blossom until during and after Nero's time, but his views and the overall anguish of the era reveal the extent to which one of Rome's greatest minds shared Paul's concern for transcendence, as well as the call of its character-molding ideals.

---

6. Marcel, *Man Against Mass Society*, 128.
7. Ibid.
8. Ibid., 131.

Transcendence and Fulfilment

Seneca's life was not without disappointment, setbacks, and moral problems. Much has been written about him (ca. 4 BCE–65 CE), his exile during Claudius' reign, and his tutorial years in service to Nero. Any number of sources may be researched to ferret out his years. But what makes Seneca of interest is his disappointment concerning Roman morals and the decay of the Empire's elite, of which he was a member. In providing his lists of moral ills, Paul was echoing the concern of many like-minded contemporaries.

It is in Seneca's collected letters, published as moral essays, that we capture a glimpse of the moral challenge that faced Paul as well as Rome. In his letter of 49 CE, composed and sent to his friend Paulinus and entitled *De Brevitate Vitae*, or "On the Shortness of Life," Seneca lists numerous indictments similar to Paul's that Seneca viewed as "perverse." The essay's title clearly acknowledges life's swift and passing brevity, but that is not Seneca's focus. It is what humankind does during its brief earthly years that matters: "Life is long enough," he writes, "but when it is squandered in luxury and carelessness, . . . devoted to no good end," then that is when humankind must take notice, though so few do. Along with Paul, Seneca laments that the world is obsessed with "avarice," shows "a toilsome devotion to tasks that are useless," is "besotted with wine," "paralyzed by sloth," "exhausted by ambition," "driven by . . . greed," "tormented by a passion for war," and "in servitude in a thankless attendance upon the great," marked by "foolish joy in greedy desire." Then, his capstone statement, Seneca declares: "You have all the fears of mortals and all the desires of immortals." Has anyone ever put this truth so bluntly and painfully? Seneca marvels that his "peers" could be so self-deceived. He goes on: "But among the worst I count also those who have time for nothing but wine and lust," "possessed by the empty dream of glory," "avaricious . . . and wrathful." To which he adds another inimitable capsheaf: "It takes the whole of life to learn how to live, and . . . it takes the whole of life to learn how to die."[9] We could cite more examples, but Seneca's despair for his own culture powerfully attests to Paul's assessment of the same. In this regard, the two thinkers longed

---

9. Seneca, *Moral Essays*, 2:289–305.

7. Pillar Four: Apollonian Restraint in a Dionysian Age

for a "redemption" of "insight" and "maturity" that in Seneca's judgment only philosophy could provide, whereas in Paul's belief, only God in Christ Jesus can make possible.

In that light, let us return to Paul and his quest for God's universal values that transform life.

8. Pillar Five: Toward Universals That Transform Life

The Apostle Paul knew that the excesses of human frailty, along with the defects of inner discord, could never liberate a person from the prison house of his or her soul. Spiritual liberation required far more, which Paul's in-Christ mysticism enabled him to grasp and proclaim.

It is interesting to note that Paul was not the only first-century Christian engaged in this pursuit. Immediately after Paul's career and martyrdom, the writer of Colossians built on Paul's identical view. Appealing to the apostle's in-Christ mysticism, he urged his readers to "set [their] minds on things that are above, not on things that are on the earth, for you have died, and your life is hidden with Christ in God" (Col 3:2–3). Thus, he goes on to advise:

> Put to death, therefore, whatever in you is earthly: fornication, impurity, passion, evil desire, and greed . . . These are the ways you also once followed, . . . But now you must get rid of all such things: anger, wrath, malice, slander, and abusive language . . . seeing that you have stripped off the old self with its practices and have clothed yourselves with the new self, which is being renewed in knowledge according to the image of its creator. (Col 3:5–10)

Then, sounding as if he were quoting from Paul's Letter to the Galatians, he adds: "In that renewal there is no longer Greek and Jew, circumcised and uncircumcised, barbarian, Scythian, slave and free; but Christ is all and in all" (Col 3:11). One simply cannot

8. Pillar Five: Toward Universals That Transform Life

continue to live immersed in one's former ways once one becomes crucified with Christ and enrobed in Christ's risen self.

Less than forty years later, the author of the *Didache* would reiterate the same. The perverse world around the young church had hardly abated. Nor had the kingdom come, as its first-century followers had hoped to witness. All the existential fears of death, dread, and Nothingness haunted the beleaguered times. Dated between 100 and 130 CE, its doctrine of "The Two Ways" appears to have been used as a "moral catechism" for new converts as well as an ecclesiastical manual for the early church. Its "two ways" are known as "the way of life" versus "the way of death." The latter draws heavily on Paul's Letter to the Romans (1:29–31) and his Epistle to the Galatians (5:19–21). Writes the author:

> But the way of death is this: First of all, it is wicked and thoroughly blasphemous: murders, adulteries, lusts, fornications, thefts, idolatries, magic arts, sorceries, robberies, false witness, hypocrisies, duplicity, deceit, arrogance, malice, stubbornness, greediness, filthy talk, jealousy, audacity, haughtiness, boastfulness. (*Did.* 5.1)[1]

In a stunning departure from Paul's letters, however, the *Didache* quotes numerous passages from the emerging gospels that were making it into "print" and circulating among the churches. As such, the *Didache* quotes the words of Jesus pertaining to the higher virtues that a person in Christ should want to incarnate. Unfortunately for Paul, he did not have a single gospel manuscript before him. He had to rely essentially on what Christ's Spirit, or a life in Christ, might have suggested he deduce. This makes for a critical difference because, in contrast, the writings of the gospels introduce believers to the historical Jesus in all his personality. They injected his presence and quasi-mystical form into their otherwise ordinary existence, as opposed to Paul's simple propositional statements and hortatory calls to virtue. That Christianity survived its first-century beginnings may have had more to do with the appearance of the written gospels than Paul's in-Christ mysticism,

---

1. *Didache*, 173.

yet without Paul's preparatory letters and his grasp of the universal meaning of the historical Jesus' appearance in time, the gospels' "lives of Jesus" would have been void of the philosophical and ontological substratum that made Christ's life worth recording. Otherwise, Jesus would have been just another "prophet" whose denunciations of the Jewish ruling classes and popularity among the people would have faded after Jerusalem's fall in 70 CE.

It is this likely "fact" that we need to remember in evaluating Paul's own quest for enduring values. The author of the *Didache*, having cited so many of Paul's warnings against a life of excess and defect, was thus able to inject new life and spirit in his readers' lives by quoting the "very words" of Jesus. In contrast to the "way of death," the "way of life" is therefore a call to an ethic based on the historical Jesus' grasp of God's norms to encourage a more perfect self-actualization:

> Now, this is the way of life: "First, you must love God who made you, and second, your neighbor as yourself." And whatever you want people to refrain from doing to you, you must not do to them . . . What these maxims teach is this: "Bless those who curse you," and "pray for your enemies." Moreover, fast "for those who persecute you." For "what credit is it to you if you love those who love you?" . . . But "you must love those who hate you," and then you will make no enemies. (*Did.* 1.2)[2]

At this point, the author goes on to cite additional sayings from Jesus' Sermon on the Mount and Sermon on the Plain, as drawn from Matthew and Luke's accounts, respectively.

This brings us back to Colossians, and to its author's call for Christ's followers to set their "minds on things that are above" (Col 3:2). Thus, the author writes: "As God's chosen ones, holy and beloved, clothe yourselves with compassion, kindness, humility, meekness, and patience. Bear with one another and . . . forgive each other; just as the Lord has forgiven you, so you must forgive" (3:12–13).

---

2. Ibid., 171.

8. Pillar Five: Toward Universals That Transform Life

Whether Paul was its author or only someone writing in his name, we may never know. Contemporary scholarship considers the letter non-Pauline, though its author knew Paul's mind-set and style inside and out. Regardless, its echo of Paul's in-Christ mysticism and quest for wholeness is beyond dispute.

Returning to Galatians, what are the "fruit[s] of the Spirit," if we may pluralize them, that capture the essence of a life hidden in Christ? And what bearing do they have as universal injunctions appropriate for our time?

First, Paul's list. He writes: "the fruit of the Spirit is love [*agapē*], joy [*chara*], peace [*eiréna*], patience [*makrothumia*], kindness [*chrastotas*], generosity [*agathosuna*], faithfulness [*pistis*], gentleness [*prautas*], and self control [*egkrateia*]. There is no law [*nomos*] against such things" (Gal 5:22–23). Paul would go on to devote an entire paragraph to agape, referring to joy eighteen times, to peace twenty-two times, to patience six times, to kindness eight times, to generosity five times, to faithfulness two times (plus four instances of the word "faithful"), to gentleness five times, and to self-control four times. All seven of Paul's genuine letters contain his opening greeting, "Grace to you and peace."

If we ask, "Why these?" the answer is simple. They constitute the vested attributes of the Holy Spirit. In addition, for Paul, if one is a follower in Christ, then the marks of the Spirit will become manifest in one's life. For some it may take years, as it probably did for Paul; for others, it might occur spontaneously, as was likely the case with Barnabas, or lead to a gradual transformation, as it did in the lives of John, Mark, Silas, Apollos, Aquilla, and so many others identified throughout Paul's letters. As marks of the Spirit, they are all facets of Paul's encouragement to his Philippians converts "to work out your salvation with fear and trembling; for it is God who is at work in you" (2:12).

For Paul, there is no *nomos*, no law, no citation of indictment, nor any preventative injunction from practicing each one of these every day, whether in public or private, quietly or in the busy agora of civil existence. They are Paul's version of Jesus' "salt of the earth" and "light of the world" admonishments. They represent intentions and actions that manifest the reality of God's kingdom at work both now and in the end time. Above all, they are without the "curse" that came with the "Law," which was seized by the elemental spirits, thus turning its God-intended goodness into a vessel of human opprobrium and condemnation.

In themselves, they are void of "excess" or "defect." Like Aristotle's virtues of the mean, they constitute the right thing to do, at the right time, in the right manner, for the right reason. They pose a challenge for all of Paul's in-Christ followers to appropriate. In that respect, they constitute a daily guide—a lifestyle to be cultivated and cherished not for oneself alone, but as values in and of themselves, applicable to all and beneficial for all.

Similar to Plato's high "ideals," they serve as attributes of God's Spirit that belong ontologically to all of Abraham's offspring, including Jew and Gentile, free and enslaved, male and female alike. However, whereas in Plato's case the "ideal forms" of the Good are accessible only by intellectual ascent, for Paul they are the mystical gifts of faith that link one's unique self to the very spiritual nature of God. To incarnate them as well as see them manifest in the lives of others belongs to the new Order of the Spirit.

Furthermore, they are not reserved for the righteous alone, nor only for the saintly, for they are God's "gifts" to everyone. It is only when we perceive them in this way that they cease to be "goals." Rather, they serve as marks of one's existential vitality to be incarnated *now* with humility and courage, however awkwardly one may fulfill them in one's present "tabernacle" of *soma* and *pneuma*. This is their greatness for Paul.

What is equally remarkable is their spirit, their comforting essence. Words like "patience," "gentleness," "love," "kindness," and "peace" create inner calm, a sense of equanimity, grace, wellbeing, and self-control that naturally influences one's behavior toward others as well. They are void of bitterness, self-deceit, vainglory, or any craving of lust or power. They speak of that "order of the Spirit" that Marcel urges humankind to attain, rather than lapsing into the orders of materialism and technology that curtail, if not silence, the invitation that life's mystery beckons us to explore.

8. Pillar Five: Toward Universals That Transform Life

Even more so, they compel pursuers—through even a cursory critique of Paul's life—to mull anew the power of his in-Christ mysticism to transform one's existence not for the worse, but for the better, both for oneself and *le monde cassé*.

It is interesting to compare Paul's Galatians list of the marks of the Spirit with Aristotle's table of preferred virtues. Rather than succumbing to the vices of either excess or deficiency, Aristotle offered the following virtues for attaining a more perfect life:

> Courage (*tharsos*) instead of bravado or cowardice;
>
> Self-control (*sophron*) instead of self-indulgence or insensitivity;
>
> Generosity (*agathosuna*) instead of extravagance or stinginess;
>
> Magnificence (*megaloprepeia*) instead of vulgarity or miserliness;
>
> High-mindedness (*megalopsychia*) instead of vanity or small-mindedness;
>
> Gentleness (*prautas*) instead of short-temperedness or apathy;
>
> Truthfulness (*spoudaios*) instead of boastfulness or self-deprecation (*eironeia*);
>
> Pleasantness instead of buffoonery or boorishness;
>
> Friendliness instead of obsequiousness and grouchiness;
>
> Shame instead of mortification or shamelessness;
>
> Righteous indignation instead of envy or spite.[3]

The above have to do with character, with excellence (*arête*), and with personal as well as civil virtues. They support Paul's appreciation of his own era's prized virtues. This sense of unity with the highest hopes of Paul's cultural timeframe appears powerfully in his Philippians appeal.

---

3. Aristotle, *Nicomachean Ethics*, bks. 3–4.

Transcendence and Fulfilment

> Finally, beloved, whatever is true [*alethé*], whatever is honorable [*semna*], whatever is just [*dikaia*], whatever is pure [*hagna*], whatever is pleasing [*prosphilé*], whatever is commendable [*euphéma*], if there is any excellence [*arête*] . . . think about these things. (Phil 4:8–9)

Paul's call to such an honorable life helps clarify any misgivings one might have concerning his attitude toward his Greco-Asian culture and its higher Aristotelian-Stoic values. True, Paul condemned the excesses and moral defects of his age, but he did not encourage his followers to abandon it. Yes, time was short; the end time would come soon. But Christ's Spirit is nonetheless meant to guide all, and Christ's love meant to be shared with all. In his chapter on "The Church in the World," Victor Furnish suggests that Paul's approach was ultimately one of "critical engagement," not abandonment of the world. All neighbors are to be loved in the name of Christ, and loved *now*.[4]

Perhaps nowhere does Paul expound his *universality of an honorable life* with greater clarity than in Rom 12:2–21:

> Do not be conformed to this world, but be transformed by the renewing of your minds, so that you may discern what is the will of God . . . I say to everyone among you not to think of yourself more highly than you ought to think, but to think with sober judgment . . . Let love be genuine; hate what is evil, hold fast to what is good; love one another with mutual affection; outdo one another in showing honor. Do not lag in zeal, be ardent in spirit; serve the Lord. Rejoice in hope, be patient in suffering . . . Contribute to the needs of the saints; extend hospitality to strangers . . . Live in harmony with one another; do not be haughty, but associate with the lowly, . . . take thought for what is noble in the sight of all. If it is possible, . . . live peaceably with all. (Rom 12:2–18)

We meet this same concern for a *universality of common accord* in a passage that immediately follows the above. It constitutes Paul's famous admonishment in which he validates the concept

---

4. Furnish, *Moral Teaching*, 159.

8. Pillar Five: Toward Universals That Transform Life

of *Christian citizenship*, or incorporating one's duty to honor both rulers and civil law. Such is ordained by God, in Paul's view, and is intended to uphold the common peace, enforce justice against wrongdoing, and advance "good conduct" based on the obligation of a sound "conscience." Taxes, revenue, respect, and honor are expected of every citizen, including Christians (Rom 13:1–7). Followers are not to opt out but instead to remain engaged in society at large. Therefore, Paul pleads: "Owe no one anything, except to love one another," which, while contributing to the commonwealth of all, fulfills the *nomos* itself (Rom 13:10).

Though Paul nowhere cites a single contemporary of his time whose political views might have supported his own, Paul's sense of the state's importance echoes the Greco-Roman mind of the period. For example, though Paul fails to distinguish between the various forms of government operative in the Empire, Cicero's concept of the state is mirrored in Paul's. As one who served as a proconsul in the apostle's own province, Cicero maintained that "the noblest use of virtue is the government of the Commonwealth, and the carrying-out in real action . . . all those . . . theories which philosophers discuss at every corner."[5] These theories of high virtue are essential to the laws of the state. In an eloquent appeal to his own peers, Cicero asks: "From whence comes piety, . . . religion, . . . civil law, . . . justice, faith, equity, . . . [along with] modesty, continence, the horror of baseness, the desire of praise and renown," if not from the wisest philosophical principles? All that is required is for leaders of courage and integrity to enact and enforce them.[6]

Cicero goes on to define a commonwealth as "a constitution of the entire people . . . bound together by the compact of justice, and the communication of utility." As he notes, "the human race is not a race of isolated individuals, wandering and solitary, but it is so constituted that even in the affluence of all things . . . [it spontaneously seeks society]." Hence, "a certain authority [is

---

5. Cicero, *Commonwealth*, 361.
6. Ibid.

needed] in order [for the state] to be permanent."⁷ Though he prefers a monarchy over an aristocracy or democracy—knowing that none of the above is either perfect or "essentially good"—as long as the state pursues what lies in its people's best interest, then, Cicero concludes, any constitution derived from one of the aforesaid systems of government, should be sufficient.⁸ Above all, such a society should be based on a constitution protecting everyone's liberty, which Cicero calls an "association of rights."

With respect to such an "association of rights," Cicero explains: "Since the law is the bond of civil society, and the justice of the law equal, by what rule can the association of citizens be held together, if the condition of the citizens be not equal?" To his question, Cicero replies: "For if the fortunes of men cannot be reduced to this equality," then "rights should be equal among those who are citizens of the same republic. For what is a republic but an association of rights?"⁹ Such a concept appears in Paul's own vision of the inclusiveness of God's kingdom when Paul writes: "For now that faith has come... There is no longer Jew or Greek, ... slave or free, ... male and female, for all are one in Christ" (Gal 3:25–28). That the Empire had not achieved Cicero's dream of a "perfect" republic did not, for Paul, negate *the spiritual rights* of all to enjoy God's benefits now—whether slave or free.

Humanity's quest for honorable, conscionable, and civil norms has not abated since Paul or Cicero's time. What is just and honorable for one age has not always been hailed "fair" for its successor. The same is true of definitions of "honorable." Yet Paul's search for a personal ethic that concomitantly upgrades a culture's quest for decency and order remains a challenge to this day. To live by less than the highest norms that society can set is to fall prey to the lowest forms of modern idolatry that exalt the worst of human frailty and spiritual discord. Voices like Marcel's are needed, along with Heidegger's, Sartre's, Camus', the Dalai Lama's, or even Nietzsche's. The same holds true for Bentham's, Kant's,

7. Ibid., 379.
8. Ibid., 380.
9. Ibid., 383.

8. Pillar Five: Toward Universals That Transform Life

Pascal's, Luther's, or Erasmus', as well as for Augustine's, Aristotle's, and Plato's. Not to mention numerous others back to the time of the Buddha's *Dhammapada* and the rishis' commentaries on the *Upanishads*.

All of which brings us to Paul's supreme, greatest virtues of all: faith, hope, and love.

Let us take love first. Though Bornkamm rejects any suggestion that Paul's ethic was influenced in any way by his mystical insight, he unfolds Paul's concept of love with deft sensitivity. For Bornkamm, Paul's concept of love meant loving one's neighbor in the fullest Hellenistic Jewish sense—that is, reaching out in a love embracing all humankind. Bornkamm reminds us that the words "to love" (*agapan*) and "love" (*agapē*), though not foreign in classical Greek, were considered subservient and insignificant to *eros* and *philia*. But not so in the Septuagint. Though he does not spell this out, a reading of the latter will reveal that its translators replaced the Hebrew *'a-both* or *'a-havot* ("love") with "agape" or past-tense forms such as *agapéseis* or *agapesa* in texts like Ps 118:159 (Gr. version) or Deut 6:5: *Kai agapéseis Kurious 'o Theou*, or "And thou shalt love the LORD thy God . . . "

Drawing on Rom 5:8, "But God showed his love for us in that while we were still sinners Christ died for us," and on Rom 8:31, "For I am persuaded that [nothing] in all creation can separate us from the love of God in Christ Jesus," Bornkamm focuses on the spiritual depth of love's meaning—that it "reaches out beyond the individual and takes in others as well."[10] In doing so, agape replaces the *eros* and/or *philia* ("friendship") that Aristotle so prized, as it exceeds both in every way. In the final analysis, agape is the essence of one's new creation.

Bornkamm considers Paul's "hymn in praise of love" as agape's best expansion, in which love is viewed as the highest gift of all God's gifts of the Spirit. It incorporates the very power of God, if not the hidden essence of God. In Bornkamm's paraphrase of Paul's 1 Cor 13:4-7 passage, God's gift of love "lasts the course, and waits for others; it does not boil over in passion; does not

10. Bornkamm, *Paul*, 216.

swagger or puff itself up; does not ignore the limits set by good manners; . . . is full of joy; . . . it rejoices in the truth that benefits others. Its force is a confidence that nothing can destroy; . . . . [Nor can it ever] fall into resignation and despair."[11]

It is this love that will conquer the world, as well as sustaining the faithful as they await the end time. From Paul's perspective, it is this love that is superior to all forms of universal value that, however noble, fail to create a new being whose interiority no longer belongs to itself but to God.

As for *faith*, Paul's passage in Rom 1:17 and elsewhere clarifies that *faith* is anchored in God's promise of free grace to Abraham and to his offspring. It rests on complete trust in God. It is not a power that humankind can claim as its own; rather, it rises in response to what God does to redeem human lives. It is anchored in one's deep trust that God's will and actions, promises and ends, have prevailed in history and will prevail for all time.

As in the story of Abraham, so it is too in the life of Paul—faith is not without its challenges, its moments of incommunicable silence and hope, of abasement and want, and even of suffering and trials and the Dark Night of the Soul. Nothing, however, can separate faith's confident conviction that God's love has, does, and will triumph in the end; indeed, it is active now in one's new life in Christ, who is the highest manifestation of God's love.

Such faith and love form the cornerstone of humankind's *hope*. Because the Eternal has cloaked itself in time and pointed the way to fulfillment, hope can clothe itself in courage to press on toward life's upward call rather than settle for doubt or its tempting cousins: disparagement, cynicism, and desperation.

In our own time, the continuing search for an ethical system based on the highest norms of universal appeal has been offered by many (Kant, Bentham, Mill, etc.). Most recently, it has been expounded and defended by the British philosopher W. D. Ross in his theory of prima facie overriding duties. Granted, they come to us without the luster of Christ's open grace; nonetheless, they capture something of those eternal first-right duties that instinctively

11. Ibid., 218.

8. Pillar Five: Toward Universals That Transform Life

come to mind. For Ross, life is such that we are often forced to choose between recognized duties, selecting the one that appears to be an "overriding duty" under the circumstances. He emphasizes seven: fidelity, reparation, gratitude, justice, beneficence, self-improvement, and non-maleficence.[12]

More specifically, *fidelity* involves the duty to honor promises and agreements (explicit or implicit) under which one has obligated oneself. This virtue is primary, if not the most important, as it undergirds the remaining six. Once broken, the other six virtues are weakened. Fidelity is reminiscent of the first commandment, "Thou shalt have no other gods before me," and all other instances where vows of faithfulness are critical (explicit or implied).

Reparation is as old as the *lex talionis*, mirrored in the Old Testament's "Leviticus Code," as well as in Hammurabi's Amorite Code. Reparation underscores the duty to repay damages and engage in restitution for wrongful acts inflicted on others. It is the central vertebra of all civil law and the anchor that stabilizes personal agreements.

Gratitude acknowledges one's debt to others for services or favors rendered as well as expressing gratefulness for all acts of kindness one receives. As an attitude, it reveals the essence of one's soul as it flows from the heart of one's character. It flows from the deepest wells of the self and comes closest to capturing Jesus' passage in Luke 6:27: "Love your enemies, do good to those who hate you, bless those who curse you, pray for those who abuse you." Such a gracious view of life has no equal and undergirds Ross' remaining virtues.

Justice manifests concern for fairness and the duty to redress any wrongdoing or harm done to others. It is central to every code of ethics as far back as humanity can trace its origins.

Beneficence recognizes an inner sense of obligation to help others in order to improve their condition and/or alleviate suffering and pain. Jesus' parable of the Good Samaritan is founded on

---

12. Lockhart, "W. D. Ross's Moral Theory." See also Ross, *Right and the Good*, 19ff.

this principle. Along with *gratitude*, it comes closest to capturing Paul's concept of love.

Self-improvement is instrumental to the edification of both the self and society, to one's self-fulfillment and ability to serve as a resource to others. Socrates considered it a hallmark virtue in his *Apology*. Self-improvement underlies all calls to greatness, and its absence undermines our noblest efforts.

Finally, *non-maleficence* is equally innate and springs from the desire not to be hurt by others, thus issuing in the duty to refrain from hurting them. Hillel of Jesus' era expressed it in his statement, "Do not do to others what you would not want them to do to you." Kant would reify it in his categorical imperative to "act in every situation as to treat others as ends and never as means."

In the multicultural and pluralistic society that dominates most Western nations, Ross' prima facie virtues are sound reminders of the marks of that "Order of the spirit" that both Paul and Marcel would encourage society to incarnate. They serve as portals of the Transcendent as well as aspects of a "spiritual consciousness" that can do more to transform lifestyles than vitalism's emphasis on "living life as it is," short of its highest order: God.

9. Pillar Six: The Delay of the Angels

"For the Lord himself, with a cry of command, with the archangel's call and with the sound of God's trumpet, will descend from heaven, and the dead in Christ will rise first. Then *we who are alive, who are left*, will be caught up in the clouds together with them to meet the Lord in the air; and so we will be with the Lord forever" (1 Thess 4:16–17).

"For the Son of Man is to come with his angels in the glory of his Father, . . . Truly I tell you, *there are some standing here who will not taste death* before they see the Son of Man coming in his Kingdom" (Matt 16:27–28).

"But *about that day or hour no one knows*, neither the angels in heaven, nor the Son, but only the Father. Beware, keep alert, for you do not know when the time will come" (Mark 13:32–33).

"Now concerning the times and the seasons, . . . you do not need to have anything written to you. For *you yourselves know very well that the day of the Lord will come like a thief in the night* . . . So then let us not fall asleep as others do, but let us keep awake and be sober" (1 Thess 5:1–2, 6).

The eschaton, or end time, did not occur for *anyone then alive* to be caught up in the clouds to meet the Lord. Nor did anyone standing and listening to Jesus' "End Time Sermon" live to see the Son of Man coming in his kingdom as he predicted, at least not in the cataclysmic way they anticipated. Even Paul suspected as much, though he kept it in the back of his mind, hoping he would live to see it but remaining vigilant all the while. The hope was part of a larger vision, inspired as far back as the time of Isaiah, when Judah's Messiah-King would finally subdue all nations and the entire world would enjoy "endless peace" with "justice and righteousness" (Isa 9:7), as the earth came to "overflow with the knowledge of the Lord as the waters cover the sea" (Isa 11:9). It was a magnificent vision, and it still is. But it did not happen, nor has it occurred to date. Time has moved on. And the world still awaits the trumpet's sound, as the angels mark time and look on.

Its delay is what forced Heidegger to launch his *Existence and Being* or *Sein und Zeit* and his concept of beingness as *Dasein*. This delay is now woven into our *da-sein*, or our being-here, thus making us captive to time and death. Nowhere does Heidegger describe this better than in his book of collected essays titled *Poetry, Language, Thought*.

As is well known, Heidegger considered Hölderlin's famed poem "Bread and Wine" to contain an insight so penetrating that he could never let go of it. It is the poet's line: "and what are poets for in a destitute time?" This word "time," claims Heidegger, "means the era to which we ourselves still belong." For Hölderlin, he notes, "the appearance and sacrificial death of Christ mark the beginning of the end of the day of the gods. Night is falling." Indeed, since the time that Heracles, Dionysus, and Christ "left the world, the evening of the world's age has been declining toward its night." Hence, their failure to arrive signals the phenomenon of "the default of God." God's default means "that no god any longer gathers men and things unto himself, visibly and unequivocally, and by such gathering disposes the world's history and man's sojourn in it." God's default "forebodes something even grimmer . . . [that] the divine radiance has become extinguished in the world's history." It is this time of the world's night, thereby, that constitutes its "destitute" condition.[1]

Even worse, God's default means that the world has lost its "ground that grounds it." Only its groundlessness remains, as its

---

1. Heidegger, *Poetry*, 89.

9. Pillar Six: The Delay of the Angels

Abgrund has fallen away, leaving an abyss in its place. Consequently, humankind cannot help but "experience" and "endure" the world's night, which has become its destitute time. Still, there clings a memory of the god Dionysus' presence as, likewise in remembrance of the sacrificial Christ, he comes back to us in bread and wine. But this he does only at night, when our feelings of destitution plummet to their lowest. Yet it is while remaining close to this abyss that we are "touched by [the] presence [of] the ancient name of Being." Here in this abyss, traces of the divine once more minister to humankind, which the wine god brings down "to the godless amidst the darkness of their world's night."[2]

What, then, are human beings to do? And of what grace and promise do its poets serve? They sing the wine god's song, and sensing "the trace of the fugitive gods, stay on the gods' tracks, and so trace for their kindred mortals the way toward the turning."[3] That is how the wine god's poets keep humankind close to Being and thus enable them to discover anew the meaning of Being and of their place in nature, both for themselves and others.

In Heidegger's mind, however, modern humankind are scarcely aware of their loss of Being, let alone of the default of God. Drawing upon Rilke and his *Duino Elegies* and *Sonnets to Orpheus*, Heidegger argues that as mortals we hardly recognize our own mortality—that we are here only briefly, once and never again—"*Einmal und nicht mere,*" to quote Rilke—and thus we fail to claim ownership of our being. So what are poets for? They sing the wine god's song in holy night, until we awaken to seize upon the meaning and purpose that our lives can have, if only we will but do so.[4]

True, this is poetry, metaphor, and metaphysics in disguise, but so is Paul's language and vision of the end time. The "default" of the Christ's return, or the angels' delay, required his quest for a solution as much as it requires ours. Paul, however, would not be defeated. He would not accept Christ's "default" as a defeat but as a time for promoting the kingdom of God, *now*. As he writes

2. Ibid., 90.
3. Ibid., 91–92.
4. Ibid., 94.

concerning the coming resurrection, when all shall be transmuted into imperishable beings: "Therefore, my beloved, be steadfast, immovable, always excelling in the work of the Lord, because you know that in the Lord your labor is not in vain" (1 Cor 15:58). Paul repeated the same charge in his Letter to the Romans, but in a far more vigorous form: "Let love be genuine; . . . Do not lag in zeal . . . Rejoice in hope, be patient in suffering, persevere in prayer . . . Bless those who persecute you; . . . Live in harmony with one another; . . . Do not repay evil for evil. If it is possible, . . . live peaceably with all" (Rom 12:9–18).

This was his answer to the "divine default" of his time. It was meant to empower his followers with hope in their own destitute time as they waited out the angels' delay until Christ could consummate the kingdom and usher in the end time.

Western culture, however, is not alone in facing the delay of the angels. The Japanese writer Yukio Mishima also addressed the "default of God" as brilliantly as Heidegger. Born in 1925 only to take his life in 1970, Mishima confronted post-war Japan with a demanding review of its values. Descended of Samurai ancestors and devoted to a mix of Shinto and Buddhist principles, he stunned the Japan of his time with a critical review of its ancient virtues in its post-war decline. His four-volume novel, *The Sea of Fertility*, traces the history of a family whose central character's (Shigekuni Honda) belief in reincarnation inspires, yet destroys him in the end. Along the way, the ancient values of loyalty to Japan's emperor, devotion to duty, faithfulness to the venerable gods of Shinto spiritualism, and Honda's own high demand for purity and concern for the poor carries the reader through his rise from a dedicated student and friend of the famed Matsugae family to become one of post-war Japan's wealthiest and most respected jurists. But similarly to Tolstoy's Ivan Ilych, Honda discovers in his declining years that he has lived for all the wrong reasons. Sacrifice, violence, passion, love, deception, perversity, and power make their debut along the way. Mishima's story captures the reality of modernity in its quest for wholeness, but it is a quest that fails. It is a modern

9. Pillar Six: The Delay of the Angels

tragedy in the order of ancient Greece's great playwrights' vision of justice denied and a life scarred by the unfulfilled. Rather than seizing upon an authentic life of his own, Honda keeps hoping to find it in the reincarnated lives of the Matsugaes and other families and persons he has come to admire. Mishima fully understood that such a quest can never be enough.

Paul's journey of becoming stands in stark contrast, as it offers humanity a vision of a life fulfilled in obedience to Being—to a Transcendent Reality of the Order of the Spirit that only unification with the Highest can make possible. But one has to "die" to one's old self to receive the life of that Other that creates a "new being." Mishima understood that and sacrificed himself to awaken his own culture's awareness of their need to become "new beings." His act of self-immolation came as a shock to his guests as they beheld in horror his blade sweep across his abdomen, just beneath his ribs.

Of course, one can exist in such a way as to deny that God's angels will ever return. A humanism void of God, or even skepticism, may take that route. But in doing so, one assumes the risk of one's own life entering into default and the loss of any hope of meaning—now or in the future. Neither Paul nor Mishima espoused this path. Nor need contemporary humankind.

The great mystics of the past sought still another way: complete absorption into the divine. They sought it now, in their lonely hours of becoming, free from the bonds of worldly affairs. Paul understood and experienced the same temptation, but he rejected that path, choosing rather to serve the Transcendent Christ in the world now, between his Mediator's departure and promised return. The stark reality is that the latter did not occur, nor has it, nor is it likely to transpire in the physical-psychological mode Paul's era imagined. Waiting for that utopian miracle to arise has channeled many to pursue a mystical unification with the divine here and now. It can be active or passive, induced by prayer and contemplation, or the result of a sudden ecstatic entrancement.

It is this form of mysticism that Pauline scholarship denies Paul ever endorsed. But its spiritual satisfaction is a reality of the highest call and one that the great saints and mystics of all faiths have embraced. Though its appeal has dimmed in our time, its rudiments are worth remembering as aspects of an intuitive unification with God that offers catharsis and renewal. It is why von Hügel and Underhill's studies of spiritual consciousness were worth investigating a century ago, and it is also why their republication was deemed advisable.

We find the appeal of the "mystical now" examined both critically and constructively in Underhill's chapter on "The Dark Night of the Soul." Relying on studies based on the writings and experiences of Madame Guyon, Saint John of the Cross, Saint Catherine of Siena, and Suso, she catalogs trials and expectations that confront such a journey. It is not for everyone, and it borders on the pathological, if not delusional, from time to time. Yet for all that, the quest's underlining value lies in the seriousness with which it punctuates a transcendent-based life during the interim between Christ's departure and the angels' delay. This "in-between time" is the time of our own ascendancy to self-realization, or the sphere in which we are offered Marcel's "order of the Spirit" to either embrace or decline. That is why the phenomenon of spiritual consciousness remains relevant to life's in-between time. It is in this transitory period that God becomes either central or marginal to our existence, a time in which we either acknowledge God as Tillich's "ultimate Ground of Being" or as a wake-up call when confronted by reality's abyss.

Underhill notes that for the great mystics, progress in the transcendent life is often marked by periods of "lassitude" following an original episode of "illumination." That Paul experienced this phenomenon is mirrored in his verse "for we have this treasure in earthen vessels" (2 Cor 4:2). Underhill's point, however, is that such "negative" moments are psychologically normal, as no one can sustain the Ecstatic without experiencing letdown or fatigue. The Mystic Way simply oscillates "between a joyous and a painful consciousness . . . between Purgation and Illumination, and again between Illumination and the Dark Night."[5] One feels

5. Underhill, *Mysticism*, 383.

9. Pillar Six: The Delay of the Angels

"stupefied and impotent," even "incapable of . . . all prayer and all good works," distracted by the very things one has renounced. This is sound insight and need not disparage the soul. Psychologically, she argues, the "'Dark Night of the Soul' is due to the double fact of the exhaustion of an old state, and the growth towards a new state of consciousness." Such intervals are natural and often accompanied by "chaos and misery."[6] They issue in "negative states" in one's journey "between the Illuminative and the Unitive life."[7] Feelings of abandonment and, above all, of "the absence of God" are equally normal. Even the psalmist voiced as much: "My God, my God, why hast Thou abandoned me?" (Ps 22:1) Yet, as the psalmist continues, "In you our ancestors trusted . . . and you delivered them" (Ps 22:4). Periods of "aridity" are simply part of the transitioning and transmutation of one's life in God. It is a process in which, claims Underhill, one learns "to cease to be the center and circumference of one's inner life," which is never without its struggles.[8] In its highest form, the self that survives and emerges from its "Dark Night" is no longer a "separated self," but "one conscious of the illumination of the Uncreated Life," or as a new creation "whose life is *one* with the Absolute Life of God."[9]

Paul would have understood, though corrected Underhill's notion of the total absorption of one's life into God's. Yet Paul comes close to it. As he opines in Philippians: "For to me, living is Christ and dying is gain. If I am to live in the flesh, that means fruitful labor for me; and I do not know which I prefer. I am hard pressed between the two: my desire is to depart and be with Christ, for that is far better; but to remain in the flesh is more necessary for you" (Phil 1:21–23). Still, the life he now lives in the flesh he lives "by faith in the Son of God, who loved me, and gave himself for me" (Gal 2:20). Paul knew he had a task to do and could not leave his followers so abruptly, even if it had been in his power. Surely others in his era also hungered to know the radiance of the

6. Ibid., 387.
7. Ibid., 388.
8. Ibid., 397.
9. Ibid., 402.

Transcendent Christ—especially those who would die in Nero's garden, suspended as they were between Christ's departure and his hoped-for descending angels. Nor did Paul wish to escape into that wholly other mystic world that Underhill describes, *so long as he knew and believed* that God needed him in the here and now more than in God's celestial paradise of peace and love.

It is this living "here and now" that poses the spiritual person's gravest challenge. Paul would have preferred to leave this world behind and ascend to heaven, but he knew that "call" was not his to make. It belonged to another. *Marana tha, marana tha,* or "Come, Lord!" (1 Cor 16:23) was the best he could offer. It behooves us to recognize the same.

An even graver danger is to lose heart all together, to accept demise, abandonment, and moral despair as normative and definitive. It is to accept defeat and the loss of the self, if not the "Death of the Soul," as Sartre entitled his last novel in a three-volume series he wrote during Germany's occupation of Paris during World War II.

Mishima recognized it too, because of the emptiness it leaves in a self as well as in a nation. Strangely, like Sartre's title above, the title he gave the fourth and last novel in his four-volume *The Sea of Fertility* was *The Decay of the Angel*. As Honda's hopes grow dimmer, his illusions more profound, his disillusions all the greater, and his judgment weaker—ever drawing him deeper into scandal, public opprobrium, and shame—he realizes the depth of his mismanaged, if not absurd, existence as a wasted life beyond redemption.

Mishima defines his condition as a fivefold recognition of one's "angel's decay." What are its five signs, he asks—indeed, what are the signs of all decaying angels? (1) They begin with the fading of their crowns, (2) then their robes' soiled appearance, (3) then a fetid odor that seeps from under their arms; (4) then their loss of self-awareness, and (5) finally the abandonment of their adorned attendants. As Honda reflects on these graphic signs, he sinks deeper and deeper into the pit of Non-being, to

9. Pillar Six: The Delay of the Angels

his own mortification.[10] Even more poignantly, in an earlier segment, Mishima observes that few ever notice the ludicrousness of their existence until it is too late. Life's seriousness simply ceases to concern them.[11] The five signs are a powerful metaphor of not only the Buddhist doctrine of the ego's impermanence, but also of the final decay of one's self as well as one's culture. And so Mishima shocked his audience by bowing his head and putting both his and his guests' existence to the sword's edge.

Heidegger refused to draw such a demoralizing conclusion—or "alarming," if "demoralizing" is too weak a word. He recoiled equally from Nietzsche's "Death of God," inserting in its place Hölderlin's priests singing stanzas in holy night to the wine god's presence in bread and wine—whether that god be Dionysus or the Christ. In truth, it can likewise be for modern humankind, as both "gods" are metaphors for the Bread of Life and the Wine of Eternity, a gift that only the Highest Transcendence can bestow.

One of the most remarkable pieces that Heidegger—himself part poet and part priest—ever penned is his essay on a line from Hölderlin's poem "The Poet's Vocation," which Heidegger translates as *"Full of merit, yet poetically, man dwells on this earth."*[12] As profound as it is remarkable, Heidegger's insight captures Paul's yearning for the eschaton as well as the nuances of Underhill's "spiritual consciousness" that hungers for unity with the One. In *Poetry, Language, Thought*, Heidegger defines "dwelling" as characterized by four factors: "earth and sky, divinities and mortals, belonging together as one." Dwelling on the earth implies that one is already "under the sky." As such, one's past and present are already in a state of "remaining before the divinities" as "Earth is the serving bearer.... The sky is the vaulting path of the sun, ... the wandering glitter of the stars, ... the light and dusk of day."[13] The divinities beckon us back to the Godhead, with God sometimes appearing, sometimes withdrawing in his concealment. "The mortals are hu-

---

10. Mishima, *Decay*, 52.
11. Ibid., 6.
12. Heidegger, *Poetry*, 214.
13. Ibid., 147–48.

man beings... because they can die. To die means to be capable of death *as* death. Only man dies, and indeed continually, as long as he remains on earth, under the stars, before the divinities."[14] Such is the meaning of "dwelling" for mortals. As Heidegger explains in greater depth, though still in metaphorical verse:

> Mortals dwell in that they await the divinities as divinities. In hope they hold up to the divinities what is unhoped for. They wait for intimations of their coming and do not mistake the signs of their absence. They do not make their gods for themselves and do not worship idols. In the very depth of misfortune they wait for the weal that has been withdrawn ... Mortals dwell in that they initiate their own nature—their being capable of death *as* death—into the use and practice of this capacity, so that there may be a good death ... [This] in no way means to make death, as empty Nothing, the goal. Nor does it mean to darken dwelling by blindly staring toward the end.[15]

What Heidegger is arguing is hardly dissimilar from Paul's own encouragement to his followers. "Be zealous," he admonished them in his Letter to the Romans. "Be hopeful, energetic, sober-minded, and devoted to each other in love." Paul wanted followers to be engaged in the very creation of making their lives on earth as noble, good, and as open to the Spirit of God as possible. In something of an existentialist fashion, he expected them to be responsible for *creating their own history* as they "worked out their salvation with fear and trembling," insofar as God was openly working in them. Essentially, Heidegger was arguing the same. Though his language, metaphors, and metaphysical system are rooted in contemporary philosophical thought, they are couched in the mythological symbolism of classical Greece. Nonetheless, Heidegger's system still upholds transcendence, spirituality, and openness before the Eternal. These are his guiding stars for all mortals who indeed know that *they must and shall die* and therefore must strive to make their dwelling on earth as meaningful as

14. Ibid.
15. Ibid., 148–49.

9. Pillar Six: The Delay of the Angels

possible—for both themselves and for others. This is legitimizing the time between Christ's departure and his hoped-for return as a valid sphere of engagement in God's kingdom. Here there is no thought of its delay or decay. The angels will know when to sing and when to sound the trumpet and break their long-held silence with their eyes fixed on Christ as well as on the earth's mortals.

All of which brings us back, strangely enough, to von Hügel and his "over concern" of the Mystic Way. In his chapter on "Mysticism and the Limits of Knowledge," he sounds a warning that all critics of mysticism no doubt share. He lists four: (1) That the "Mystic" as a mystic, runs the error of "ignoring" and "neglecting," or tends "to over-minimize, the absolutely necessary contact of the mind and will with the things of sense," thus giving "to Mysticism . . . its shadowy character, its floating above, rather than penetrating into, reality."[16] Accordingly, (2) "the Mystic finds his full delight in all that approximates most nearly to Simultaneity, and Eternity; and consequently turns away . . . from the Successive and Temporal represented by History."[17] Still again, (3) "the Mystic finds his joy in the sense of a Pure Reception of the Purely Objective," thus creating an "antipathy to even a relative, God-willed independence and power of self-excitation," resulting in a "constant bent towards Quietism."[18] As we have seen, both Paul and Heidegger reject this "under-minimizing" of the here and now, though each is devoted to the Transcendent in different ways. Finally, (4) "the Mystic . . . finds his joy in so exciting the difference of nature between himself and God, and the incomprehensibility of God for every finite intelligence . . . to cut away all ground for any experience or knowledge sufficient to justify him in even a guess as to what God is like or is not like."[19] All this, for von Hügel, exacerbates the error of Kierkegaard's over-emphasis of God's absolute nature, in which God becomes a Being so different from humankind as

---

16. Von Hügel, *Mystical Element*, 284–85.
17. Ibid., 285.
18. Ibid., 286.
19. Ibid., 287.

to drive humankind toward "insanity."[20] Quoting one of Kierkegaard's critics of the time, he notes: "For the man who lives for God [in Kierkegaard's way] 'is a fish out of water,'" promoting a life that "abolishes all possibility of any positive relation" between God and humankind on earth.[21]

The warning is justified, lest one's concern for the angels' *delay* lapses into grief over the angels' *decay*, thus pushing humankind toward unfaith and cynicism—a temptation that neither the Apostle Paul nor the poet-metaphysician Heidegger was willing to risk.

---

20. Ibid.
21. Ibid., 288.

10. Pillar Seven: Human Fate—Fulfillment and Destiny

In the final analysis, the meaning of life is for the individual to define. Others may point the way, but each of us is responsible for our self-determination and actualization. We are each accountable for the history we write of the self, of how as individuals we each relate to the Universal as well as to the Eternal, to one another, and to the world about us. Paul's in-Christ mysticism guided him toward his own fulfillment and ontological reality as a human being "dwelling spiritually" upon the earth. Just how much of Being we are willing to appropriate in our journeys of becoming is the question we must each ask and answer on our own.

There is much that contemporary humanity faces to achieve such a challenge. This is nothing new, however, nor is it something that only we find ourselves pressed to consider. This thought should bring *comfort* in knowing that each of us is part of something infinitely antecedent, eternal—compared to our mortality— and unbegotten, ineffable, yet present in our self-consciousness as something immanently Absolute, as we measure our self-mystery against its unyielding *thereness*. It is known as the "That Thou Art" of Hinduism, the "I am that I am" of Judaism, and the Logos of both Platonism and Johannine Christianity. Each possesses an inner beauty of its own, an indestructible good, a *Dasein* knowable as its Ground of Being.

Realizing the above should instill in us *courage*, knowing that countless lives before us have struggled with the phenomenon of that inescapable *thereness* too. Recognized as immanent yet transcendent, it has haunted humankind from the dawn of our hominid ancestry, to the era of our Ice Age predecessors, and down to the present time. All one has to do is leaf back through the pages of Abraham's self-consciousness to mull his own response to the mystical nature of life's journey. Facing west of the Chaldees and having left behind his father, mother, and the land of his birth, he said "Yes" to the voice of that inner Transcendence that promised to fulfill him, wherever he sojourned until he settled down to "dwell" in Hebron by the oaks of Mamre. There he would live in gratitude and faith as well as in fear and trembling. His is a rich story, a profound archetype for any and all to ponder, which is both our privilege and our debt.

Ours may be a different time, a different era of becoming. But the human condition has not changed that extensively. Nor has our craving for ontological wholeness abetted, nurtured as it is by that Universal Consciousness that whispers our name in the "holy nights" of our souls.

Once having encountered the Living Mystical Christ, Paul was never the same. It is doubtful whether Paul sat down and created a list of goals he hoped to attain or ever puzzled over the meaning of an "unexamined life," as Socrates, Plato, and Aristotle did. The *apocalypse* of the risen Christ gave meaning and direction to all else he could imagine doing. The "unitive experience" of that moment led to a transformation of Paul's personality and career that lasted the rest of his life. He became a "new being," set free from the world orders that strove to bind his conscience, save those founded on the love of God for the good of all. More specifically, (1) the experience brought order to his life, (2) enabled him to understand his true essential nature or identity as a person, (3) clarified his allegiance to the temporal and perishable in light of the Eternal and Imperishable, and (4) guided him toward creating an ethic of benevolence and harmony for the here and now. These four aspects of Paul's transformation are worthy of elaboration.

10. Pillar Seven: Human Fate—Fulfillment and Destiny

1. An Orderly Life

Such a life inspired by God's Spirit, or even Marcel's Transcendence of the highest form, retains merit to this day. Both grace us with an illuminating perspective on how to live as well as how to engage ourselves in the world with courage and perseverance. As Paul admonishes: "If you sow to your own flesh, you will reap corruption from the flesh; but if you sow to the Spirit, you will reap eternal life from the Spirit" (Gal 6:8).

Plato would have concurred and, in fact, championed its relevance in his dialogue on Socrates' death. The latter's friends begged him to escape while he could; even his jailor concurred and agreed to assist him. No one wanted Socrates to die, much less to watch him drain the fatal cup that the Athenian Assembly had sentenced him to drink. But Socrates would no more violate his homeland's sacred laws than Jesus would disdain the cup his Father had sent him to drink by fleeing Gethsemane the night of his arrest, though he full well knew what was about to befall him.

What is the Spirit that speaks its words of truth and encouragement to modern souls today? Indeed, is anyone listening? What is it that offers stability and order amid life's crises and chaos? For many, it is no longer Christianity's Risen Jesus, or Judaism's holy Torah, let alone the Qur'an, even if the adherent is purely secular. Nor does the quietism of the Buddha, nor the quaint way of Taoism, nor even the mystical path of Zen appeal to everyone. The philosophical "Dread" of which Heidegger speaks, along with his concept of "Nothingness" and its potential to awaken us from our forfeiture, leaves many of us cold, if not stupefied. Yet Heidegger's assessment still constitutes an encounter with the mystery of the Transcendent, as it never ceases to put our existence to the question. No person or culture, individual or society, can escape its mystery; nor our awareness of its inexplicable beauty, goodness, and truth; nor our longing to be at peace with the All in all. In reflection, beauty, goodness, and truth are hardly inventions of the mind or mere intellectual "universals"; rather, they represent noetic discoveries of the human soul in its daily response to the Voice of Being.

Paul continues: "So let us not grow weary in doing what is right, for we will reap at harvest time, if we do not give up. So then, whenever we have an opportunity, let us work for the good of all" (Gal 6:9–10). Illumination, determination, and courage are part of the becoming years of our lives. They are grounded in our consciousness of the boundaries of our being, caught between the delay of the angels and that eternity which belongs to us now.

2. Ontological Identification as Persons

What does it mean to be a human being when it is all said and done, after all one's moments of self-examination have been exhausted? To whom do we pledge our hearts, if we pledge them at all? Beyond the principles that inform our cognitive grasp of the world, what of the intuitive experiences that provide insight into self-identity, as well as their directives for actions and goals? What, if anything, is ultimate and all else peripheral, however urgent or tangential one's journey may be? What defines humanity as nothing else can? Is there any reality higher than the self, or family, or one's private hopes, dreams, and aspirations? What constitutes humanity's guiding principle above all others? What can serve as a refuge when all else fails, as that hope that keeps one striving and burns as the central flame on the quiet altar of one's heart?

For Paul, it was knowing that he no longer belonged to himself but to God—that God was present in his life, giving meaning and purpose, hope and courage to all else that he undertook and, indeed, that he considered himself blessed to attain.

Paul's mystical union with Christ, or his "in-Christ mysticism," as Schweitzer so brilliantly identified it, may not be a "unitive" or even "intuitive experience" that contemporary humanity is capable of experiencing, let alone deem worth pursuing. Yet we are each linked to the universe's Ground of Being as particles of its quantum mystery, even as we are cognizant of the fact. We are facets of its grand "debris," its evolving and creative forces. We are

10. Pillar Seven: Human Fate—Fulfillment and Destiny

links in its great chain of Being, as Pseudo-Dionysius and medieval Europe's mystics and philosophers propounded. That defines *what* we are: created entities in the great chain of becoming, guests of the universe whose perishable qualities will pass away, yet whose imperishable quantum imprint will remain. That is *what* we are, but *who* we are is a facet of *our* determination, of our response to the Ineffable and Transcendent Mystery that haunts our facticity. Even in Hinduism, the abstract and universal Brahman—the sole reality underlying all else—still manifests itself as knowable in the distinct form of Saguna Brahman, or the Trinity of Brahma (creator) Vishnu (sustainer), and Shiva (pathway to death and rebirth). God is ineffable, however one defines God, and known intuitively as that sole One from whose presence our mortality can never flee (Ps 139). This is a given for every mortal: that ultimate mystery behind one's hunger for ontological wholeness that only God can satisfy, or that trust in the Highest Transcendence that enables one to attain self-realization.

Such a holistic pursuit does not come without its trials and false starts or without doubt, anxiety, and moments that witness to the forlorn absurdity of existence. Paul fully understood that, just as well as Socrates, Augustine, the Buddha, and the Dalai Lama of today. Paul enables us to articulate the depths of life's ongoing struggles, which he encapsulated in his remarkable words: "Not that I have already obtained this or have already reached the goal; but I press on to make it my own, because Christ Jesus has made me his own. Beloved, I do not consider that I have made it my own; but this one thing I do: forgetting what lies behind and straining forward to what lies ahead, I press on toward the goal for the prize of the heavenly call of God in Christ Jesus" (Phil 3:12–14).

This is every man and woman's possibility, however they define the "goal," or the "heavenly prize," or "God."

3. Between the Perishable and Imperishable

"I die every day," wrote Paul (1 Cor 15:31). As shocking as it is profound, Paul's statement rises to universal validity. The present slips by us into the past; only its memory lingers until it fades in time. That is what it means to be *mortal*, created of perishable stuff, as well as to be *human* and aware of the mystery of the Eternal in the midst of our daily dying. But the "sting of death" can only be overcome to the extent to which the perishable puts on the imperishable and the mortal the immortal, says Paul (1 Cor 15:50–55). Interestingly enough, Paul quotes a fragment of Epicurean philosophy: "Let us eat and drink, for tomorrow we die," but he does so only because the latter fails to take death seriously, rather than realizing that death is the gateway to eternity now. If we cannot give up the perishable, then there remains no room in our cup for the Eternal. Then he quotes the poet Menander: "bad company ruins good morals" (1 Cor 15:32–33).

Paul's theology of the resurrection provides the context for the above. There can be little doubt that for Paul the resurrection was an event to occur at the end time, though its spiritual significance applies now. Now is the time of the eternal life, if by that we mean God's spiritual indwelling in our present lives as we await Christ's second coming and the consummation of God's kingdom. Beyond that, Paul's development of an afterlife is couched in metaphor and quasi-metaphysical realism that hints at a kingdom of perfection on earth and results in the conquest of death and the overthrow of all the dark powers and principalities of hell. It is the time of God's triumph and the triumph of God's will. Nevertheless, all that is still vague, mystical, and a world in which humanity's perishable nature is transformed into the imperishable and immortal, signaling the end to struggle and sorrow. Paul was willing to leave it at that and claim Christ's power to transform his existence now. If anything is to be emphasized, it is that. Speculation beyond Paul's personal belief system and metaphors and into his proto-scientific views and understanding of reality leads nowhere except into fantasy, literalism, and the unreality of the human experience.

Paul's realm eludes us today, but not his words about death, life, hope, courage, or the power of an "in-Christ mysticism" to transform life. His wisdom rings with the truth of the Transcendent's capacity to make one fit for whatever future the Eternal and

10. Pillar Seven: Human Fate—Fulfillment and Destiny

Ineffable summons one to incarnate. That it comes to fruition in the lives of countless prophetic and gentle souls worldwide is hardly a mystery. It is the Mystery that redeems all mystery, the Universal that humanizes our mortal clay and lifts our interiority into the greatness of God. We know of it in its finest form only in "personality," when the Universal becomes historical as a reality in time and not merely as an abstract ideal. It is what Paul captured so powerfully and essentially in his reference to Christ, "who did not regard equality with God as something to be exploited, but emptied himself, . . . being born in human likeness . . . humbled himself and became obedient to the point of death, even death on a cross" to redeem human beings (Phil 2:6–8).

Seeking equilibrium between Being and becoming and between the Eternal and Death has long tormented the philosophical world as well as its twin: spiritual consciousness. Heidegger focused on Death because it is the one human event that cannot be out-distanced, nor can its reality be denied. Whoever cannot take Death seriously cannot understand life. Death defines the exquisite limits of life and cuts across all glib ignoring of its significance. For Heidegger, each of us "enjoys" a unique span that is like no one else's, all our own, and inseparable from our personal and individual *Dasein*—our specific and particular beingness. Its truth is as old as Jesus' statement: "unless a grain of wheat falls into the earth and dies, it cannot bear fruit" (John 12:24).

If reading David Hume's *Essay on Human Understanding* aroused the Prussian Kant out of his "dogmatic slumber," then reading Heidegger jolted Nicolas Berdyaev out of his. In his book *The Destiny of Man*, Berdyaev—Russia's equivalent to Heidegger, Kant, and Kierkegaard combined—devoted his most eloquent section to the phenomenon of "Death and Immortality." Along with Heidegger, he concurred that "Death is the most profound and significant fact of life." It lifts "the least of mortals above the mean commonplaces of life," and it alone provides depth to the question of its meaning. In fact, Berdyaev argues, life only has meaning because of death, for "if life in our world continued for ever," he notes, "there would be no meaning in it." With a touch of sarcasm, he adds that Plato "was right in teaching that philosophy was the practice of death," though philosophy itself "does not know how one ought to die and how to conquer death." The philosophic form of immortality simply cannot show the way.[1]

Belief in immortality misses the point. It is only death that manifests the depth of life. Living on and on proves nothing. As Berdyaev attempts to explain, "Life is noble only because it contains death, an end which testifies that man is destined to another and a higher life." Endless time is incapable of revealing that truth. Meaning can only be discovered in the Eternal. As he continues, "[Death] inspires in us proof that we belong not only to the surface but to the depths as well, not only to temporal life but also to eternity." It awakens in us the realization that we belong to another world and that we must die to this one to live fully in it. Thus, death carries with it not only a biological and psychological component, but a spiritual one as well.[2]

In keeping with Paul's statement: "I die every day," Berdyaev agrees that death is a facet of one's whole existence. Our existence is "full of death and dying," he notes. Life is a perpetual experience of dying, of "experiencing the end in everything, a continual judgment passed by eternity upon time."[3] Every day involves a "partial dying" of the human body and soul. The fullness of life simply cannot be achieved within the limits of space and time. Only the Eternal can do that. Space and time condemn us to "severances and separations." And within that boundary, death always wins, once again testifying that "meaning is to be found in eternity and in fullness of being."[4] We will not find it anywhere else.

Berdyaev considers his above statements as acknowledgments of Death's "positive side." But Death carries a negative side too. Every kind of evil is associated with Death. Sounding like Paul in his enumerations of human perversity, Berdyaev writes: "Murder, hatred, malice, depravity, envy, vengeance are death and

1. Berdyaev, *Destiny of Man*, 317–18.
2. Ibid., 319.
3. Ibid.
4. Ibid., 320.

10. Pillar Seven: Human Fate—Fulfillment and Destiny

the seeds of death." And along with "pride, greed and ambition are deadly in their results . . . [for] Death is the evil result of sin." How is that? Because Death "is the denial of eternity and therein lies its ontological evil, its hostility to existence, its striving to reduce creation to non-being." Therefore, Death becomes a "negative testimony to God's power and to the Divine meaning manifested in the meaningless world." In order to put an end to that meaninglessness, God had to put Death to death itself.

In agreement with Paul—though he never mentions him—Berdyaev recites the Christian tradition that God had to send his Son to die in order to destroy death and its power. Hence, through the cross, "death is transfigured and leads us to resurrection and to life." In fact, the "whole life of this world must be made to pass through death and crucifixion, else it cannot attain resurrection and eternity." Thus, Berdyaev insists with Heidegger that death must be taken seriously and not rationalized as something commonplace or within the ordinary. "Terrible as it is to admit it, the significance of life is bound up with death and is only revealed in the face of death." For this reason, struggle against death "in the name of eternal life is man's main task."[5]

For Berdyaev, the struggle against death "in the name of eternal life" implies a moral obligation. Reminiscent of Kant's categorical imperative, Berdyaev states that one must "act so as to conquer death and affirm everywhere, in everything and in relation to all, eternal and immortal life" so as to become a giver of life and radiate creative energy for everyone and everything. With something of a rhapsodic flare and ecstatic note, he adds: "Love for all that lives, for every creature, rising above the love for abstract ideas, means struggle against death in the name of eternal life."[6]

For Berdyaev, the concept of immortality as promoted by either naturalism or idealism cannot substitute for the Eternal. Humankind's spiritual being in belonging to the Eternal can only be satisfied by the victory of one's "personality," savored by God. Naturalism, idealism, materialism, and positivism cannot sustain

5. Ibid., 322.
6. Ibid.

"personality." They are too abstract, or too ideal. That is why, for Kierkegaard, the Universal had to become particular and available as a historical moment in order for individual self-consciousness to be reborn, as it was for Abraham and the apostles. Nor can a mysticism divorced from the historical reality of incarnation serve any better. Writes Berdyaev:

> Resurrection means spiritual victory over death, it leaves nothing to death and corruption, as abstract spiritualism does. The doctrine of resurrection recognizes the tragic fact of death and means victory over it—which is not to be found in any doctrines of immortality, whether Orphic or Platonic or theosophical. Christianity alone faces death, recognizes both its tragedy and its meaning, but at the same time refuses to reconcile itself to it and conquers it.[7]

In drawing his thoughts to a close, Berdyaev maintains that eternal and immortal life must be "regarded from within," not as something one enters after death. Paul would agree, though on grounds sustained by his in-Christ convictions. For Berdyaev, the eternal life differs essentially from even a "supernatural existence." As he sums it up: "[Eternal life] is a spiritual life, in which eternity is attained while still in time . . . Eternal life is revealed in time, it may unfold itself in every instant as an eternal present. Eternal life is not a future life but life in the present, life in the depths of an instant of time."[8] It is a mistake, Berdyaev warns, to conceive of eternity as futuristic, as some kind of quasi-existence beyond the grave, or as a realm we can enter only after death. "Eternity and eternal life come not in the future but in a moment, i.e. they are a deliverance from time, and mean ceasing to project life into time." Thus, "to transcend death . . . is not to forget it or be insensitive to it, but to accept it within one's spirit, so that it ceases to be a natural, temporal fact and becomes a manifestation of meaning which proceeds from eternity."[9]

7. Ibid., 328.
8. Ibid., 333.
9. Ibid.

10. Pillar Seven: Human Fate—Fulfillment and Destiny

This may be a far cry from Paul's spiritual in-Christ mysticism, let alone his "in the air" expectations based on the classical world's view of the "imperishable versus the perishable" that he had inherited. Even Cicero wondered if possibly the soul's lighter constitution of air and fire didn't naturally "ascend," whereas its heavier elements of water and earth naturally sink "downward" to perish. Nonetheless, Berdyaev's views are profound. Certainly, his theology of the Eternal Now is more in line with today's understanding of death and the Eternal than the Apostle Paul's. The latter's words rightly inspire and nurture our souls, but Berdyaev's equally speak of an illumination with the power to energize our becoming in the midst of time.

If one has any doubts about the relevance of Berdyaev's interpolation concerning the Eternal, all one has to do is recall the quandary faced by the people of Paul's era as to its meaning for them. Socrates, Epicurus, and Cicero—all three addressed the question and sought to comfort their friends' minds concerning fate and destiny.

In the *Apology*, Socrates ponders the end of life and what might lie ahead. Perhaps one simply falls asleep never to awaken again, or better still, perhaps one journeys to the realm of Zeus, where the soul may bask in the celestial joy of conversing with the gods and life's great heroes who dwell in peace. Whichever, Socrates will be pleased.

As for Epicurus, he resolved that two things fill the heart with worry and thus make present and contemporary joy impossible: the fear of the gods and the fear of death. The gods should be honored, but they should never be feared, as they indwell their own sphere and are burdened enough with matters of their own. As for death, it is merely the dissolution of the infinite, tiny, and innumerable atoms that constitute human minds and bodies. Once these perishable molecules decay and enter "death," we are no more. All pain and wonder, sorrow and fear, consciousness and sensations cease. Against the screen of that infinity, Epicurus proposed as life's meaning the quest of tranquility—not the hedonistic "eat, drink, and be merry" philosophy associated with his school of thought. On the contrary, what Epicurus proposed was a select approach of enhancing one's pleasure while avoiding pain, controlling one's desires, and seeking friendship within a community of like-minded company.

For Cicero, it is the philosophic life of wisdom, or right reason, that lifts one to the pinnacle of human destiny. As for death and eternity, his views are similar to Socrates' (or rather Plato's). In his remarkable essay "On the Contempt of Death"—written less than half a century before Paul's time—Cicero concludes concerning one's last days:

> For if that last day does not occasion an entire extinction, but a change of abode only, what can be more desirable? And if it, on the other hand, destroys, and absolutely puts an end to us, what can be preferable to the having a deep sleep fall on us, in the midst of fatigues of life, and being thus overtaken, to sleep to eternity? And should this really be the case, then Ennis's language is more consistent with wisdom than Solon's, for our Ennis says,
>
> Let none bestow upon my passing bier
> One needless sigh or unavailing tear.
>
> But the wise Solon says,
>
> Let me not unlamented die, but o'er my bier
> Burst forth the tender sigh, the friendly tear.[10]

4. Benevolence and Harmony

Paul's encounter with the Living Christ lifted him into a realm "higher" than merely the heavenly, if by "heavenly" we seek an escape from anxiety and dread. Paul was still a resident of God's created order—the earth—however dominated by perverse powers, unruly principalities, depravity, and death. As he expressed it for his Galatians' followers: "Bear one another's burdens, and in this way you will fulfill the law of Christ" (Gal 6:2). Perhaps another way of describing Paul's concern might be labeled: "toward

---

10. Cicero, *Commonwealth*, 27.

10. Pillar Seven: Human Fate—Fulfillment and Destiny

a universality of humanity," or "A new creation is everything" (Gal 6:15). Elsewhere, Paul adds, "Live your life in a manner worthy of the gospel of Christ," (Phil 1:27) and "Do all things without murmuring and arguing, so that you may be blameless [and] . . . shine like stars in the world" (Phil 2:14–15).

These are hardly the admonitions of a spiritual enthusiast determined to escape the world. Rather, Paul was a realist who, though his soul belonged to eternity, neither could nor would abandon his "Christ-appointed mission" on earth. To live in eternity meant he *also* had to *live the eternal life* while *dwelling on earth*. As we have noted earlier, he was torn between the two: "I am hard pressed between the two: my desire is to depart and be with Christ, . . . but to remain in the flesh is more necessary for you" (Phil 1:23). "If then there is any encouragement in Christ, any consolation from love, . . . any compassion and sympathy, . . . be of the same mind, having the same love, being in full accord and of one mind" (Phil 2:1–2). He continues: "Do nothing from selfish ambition or conceit, but in humility regard others as better than yourselves. Let each of you look not to your own interests, but to the interests of others" (Phil 2:3–4). Then follows Paul's incorporation into the text of (what is deemed today) the magnificent "hymn" of Christ's self-emptying, which shows that Christ, who did not count equality with God as a thing to be grasped, instead became human—even to the point of death—so that he might serve God and humanity. That is the "mind-set" that Paul longs for humanity to share, to put into action for the glory of God, and for every bended knee to hail and every tongue confess (Phil 2:10–11).

To live a life that takes part in the Eternal Now may be the greatest of all Paul's pillars of wisdom and the foundation of an ontological existence that fulfills human destiny as no other quest can.

11. Fragments, Postulates, and Recurring Questions

1. Fragments

Metaphors abound that still haunt passages of the Pauline literature. By way of fragments, we find Paul's reference to himself as a *libation*: "even if I am poured out as a libation [*spéndomai–spéndo*] over the sacrifice and the offering of your faith, I am glad and rejoice with all of you" (Phil 2:17). This "fragment" is tantalizing because it mirrors not only Paul's Hebraic ancestry, but also in this instance his Greco-Cilician background as well.

In the Old Testament, the fourth book of Moses (Numbers) considers the "libation," or "drink offering," a major component of the various purification, sin, thanksgiving, and celebratory sacrifices worthy of God. One of the earliest mentions of the drink offering, however, appears in Gen 35:11–15, the famous passage in which Jacob commemorates God's summons (—in voice) to him at El-Bethel, where, upon his return from Aram, God assures Jacob that he will bless him and make of him a great nation, just as he promised Isaac and Abraham before him. Then Jacob pours out a drink offering and oil on the stone where God spoke to him, calling the place "Bethel," meaning "the house of God."

It is in Numbers, however, that we find references to the drink offering in association with burnt offerings, sacrifices, and "freewill offerings" intended to fulfill a vow. Their purpose is to demonstrate one's own gratitude, as well as that of the twelve tribes, to God upon entering the promised land "in order to make a pleasing odor for the Lord" (Num 15:2–3). As ancient and primitive as these rituals sound, they commence that long road of future

11. Fragments, Postulates, and Recurring Questions

and refined sacrifices, offerings, and libations that the Israelites expected of themselves in order to render to God in thanks for his mighty acts of salvation. That Paul is willing to become such a libation, poured out in behalf of Christ's ministry, is a reference to far more than his own self-sacrifice. He wanted his life, not just his death, to be a pleasing libation in gratitude to God's ineffable acts of commitment to Abraham and his offspring. In this metaphor, Paul is invoking the secret of God's plan of redemption, which has been kept hidden since the foundation of the world and has now been revealed for humankind's open salvation.

The "libation," however, that Paul mentions in his Philippians passage carries a hidden meaning that at first escapes the eye. It is one his Philippians audience would have grasped immediately. Libations poured upon stone—as in the case of Jacob's ritual—were nothing new. As far back as anyone could remember, libations and drink offerings were central to the worship and honoring of the Homeric and Olympian gods. When groups met, libations of wine were poured into bowls and then poured out in honor of Zeus first; his Olympian counterparts second; the great heroes Heracles, Dionysus, and others third; then to Zeus again and to any of the other gods guests wished to honor. A common cup was often passed among the attendees as they paid their vows and offered prayers to Zeus. To conclude such rituals, wine was poured over the flames of any animal sacrifice present. The word for "libation" is roughly the same (*spendo*). Walter Burkert reminds his readers that:

> When Achilles sends Patroclus out to battle, he takes from his chest the cup from which he alone drinks, cleans it, washes his hands, and draws the wine; then, stepping into the court, he pours out the wine and, looking up to the sky, prays for the victory and safe return of his friend. Zeus grants the one prayer, but denies the other.[1]

Burkert notes that one of the more treasured urns that has survived from the classical world is a cup displaying Apollo pouring out a drink offering (*spendo*) over a stone that was known as

---

1. Burkert, *Greek Religion*, 71.

the *Omphalos*, the navel or center of the world, that served as the sacred shrine of Delphi.[2] Apollo's twin sister, Artemis, accompanies him and participates in the ritual. One could almost paraphrase Tertullian to ask, "What has Delphi to do with Bethel?" That in Christ Jesus Paul has discovered the true "navel" of the world gives an entire new meaning to his "libation" phrase.

What could be more fitting than this ancient ritual—whether preserved on a Grecian urn or memorialized on Jacob's stone—to remind all earth's inhabitants of what is the very ground of life and of the devotion that only a full heart can offer? How better to remind us that only by offering such devotion can we hope to discover the richest unity and equilibrium of existence? It represents ancient Greece's own "self-emptying" of a human life for God alone to indwell. In hindsight, Zeus was incapable of self-emptying, thus requiring Apollo to become the god of "know thyself." In Paul's mind, however, none of the Greek gods prevailed, or else he would have claimed them over his "Christ Jesus."

There are other fragments that seize our consciousness and conscience as well. "But God . . . set me apart before I was born and called me through his grace . . . to reveal his Son to me" (Gal 1:15–16). Paul never thought of himself as belonging to or defined by the exigencies of time alone, but rather as belonging to all time—indeed, to the Creator of time itself, whose love and will alone illuminate present time and clarify the depth of existence. The specifics of the latter may differ for each of us, but not the arena in which God's transcendent dream embraces all.

Likewise, Paul's references to athletic events, such as his allusion to the runner's race also mentioned in his Letter to the Philippians, deserve consideration. "Not that I have already obtained . . . the goal; but I press on to make it my own . . . I press on toward the goal for the prize of the heavenly call of God in Christ Jesus" (Phil 3:12–14).

The symbolism of athletic competition is all the greater spelled out in his Letter to the Corinthians, where Paul admonishes Christ's followers with these words:

---

2. Ibid., 72.

11. Fragments, Postulates, and Recurring Questions

> Do you not know that in a race the runners all compete, but only one receives the prize? Run in such a way that you may win it. Athletes exercise self-control in all things; they do it to receive a perishable wreath, but we an imperishable one. So I do not run aimlessly, nor do I box as though beating the air; but I punish my body and enslave it, so that after proclaiming to others I myself should not be disqualified. (1 Cor 9:24–27)

These texts are worth citing because Judaism forbade its athletes from participating in athletic competitions in which runners dressed scantly or raced naked, as would have been the case in the experience of Paul's audience. On the contrary, Paul's allusions ignore such restrictions, suggesting that he well understood the appeal of the Greco-Asian competitions and either deliberately or inadvertently welcomed such illustrations to advance his cause.

It further haunts us to remember that Paul, though reluctant at times, refers to physical limitations of his own. Were they congenital birth defects? Had he once been a runner or boxer and competed in athletic events, now only to be sidelined due to injuries or disabilities acquired along the way? It makes one ponder. Paul hints of these in his Letters to the Galatians and Corinthians. "You know that it was because of a physical infirmity that I first announced the gospel to you; though my condition put you to the test, you did not scorn or despise me" (Gal 4:13–14). And again in 2 Cor 12:7: "Therefore to keep me from being too elated, a thorn was given me in the flesh, a messenger of Satan to torment me, to keep me from being too elated." Do the words "scorn" and "despise" provide clues as to why Paul defends his "authority" again and again?

Nonetheless, Paul was of this world, this world of Greco-Asian culture was, though he rarely emphasizes it, always present in his mind. Rather than detracting from his understanding of Christ Jesus, it enriches it for those who have eyes to see and ears to hear what Paul's Spirit is saying: that the Palestinian Jesus of Peter and James is equally the Savior of the Greco-Roman world. Decoding that message today constitutes a continuing spiritual challenge.

2. Postulates

There are *postulates* that emerge in the process of Paul's theological development that deserve mention. We find them mainly in the collection that scholarship has designated as the "non-Pauline epistles," principally Ephesians and Colossians. In both instances, however, the questionable material consists of views compatible with earlier positions of Paul's, yet taken to "extremes" in Ephesians and Colossians.

In Ephesians, three sets of verses in particular seem incompatible with Paul's earlier views: (1) The first concerns the "mystery of [God's] will . . . as a plan for the fullness of time, to gather up all things in [Christ], things in heaven and things on earth" (Eph 1:8-10). This mystery motif is further expanded in Eph 3:3-10, where Paul mentions the word "mystery" no less than four times in reference to "the plan . . . hidden for ages in God." For contemporary scholarship, this theme introduces an *overt philosophical* position that Paul generally understates. For Paul, the "fullness of time" still lies ahead, though Christ has inaugurated it.

(2) So too is the enlargement of Paul's original position on salvation through faith, which is now to include the notion of "grace" as a "gift," and not as a willed leap of faith, per Abraham. "For by grace you have been saved through faith, and this is not your own doing; it is the gift of God" (Eph 2:8). Granted, grace is a gift—a gift bestowed apart from "the results of work, so that no one may boast." Thus, the verse appears to add a nuance not overtly emphasized in Galatians or Romans. True, the position is very close to Paul's, if not a valid logical postulate; nonetheless, Pauline scholars are reluctant to view it as his. In any event, Christian doctrine has adopted it as a primary position, especially among theologians of Reformed churches.

(3) Finally, a third group of statements in Ephesians pertain to an ecclesiastical vision much larger than any Paul could have conceived: "There is one body and one Spirit, just as you were called to the one hope of your calling, one Lord, one faith, one

11. Fragments, Postulates, and Recurring Questions

baptism, one God and Father of all, who is above all and through all and in all" (Eph 4:4-6).

As for Colossians, a major postulate appears that also expands Paul's mystical view of Christ. It pertains to the writer's *further divinization of the human Jesus*, or Paul's designated Son of God and descendant of the house of David. Writes Colossians' author: "He is the image of the invisible God, the firstborn of all creation, for in him all things in heaven and on earth were created, things visible and invisible, whether thrones or dominions or rulers or powers—all things have been created through him and in him. He himself is before all things, and in him all things hold together" (Col 1:15-16). These laurels, however, are but a preamble for his culminating claim: "For in him *all the fullness of God* was pleased to dwell, and through him God was pleased to reconcile to himself all things, whether on earth or in heaven" (1:19-20). Yes, the seeds of these thoughts are Pauline, yet they witness to a process that would elevate Jesus to the highest realm of transcendence itself—a realm Paul hesitates to glorify at the expense of God the Father.

These are genuine postulates and need not be rejected; nevertheless, they attest to the early church's struggle with accommodating itself to Paul's influence as well as wrestling with the mysterious and compelling life of the historical Jesus, to whom the gospel writers would soon turn. This needs to be cited, for as Crossan has so keenly observed: *"If you begin with Paul, you will interpret Jesus incorrectly; if you begin with Jesus, you will interpret Paul differently."*[3] Crossan's judgment is hardly an overstatement. It justifies why a critique of Paul's pillars of wisdom is warranted in emphasizing his Greco-Asian background as much as his Hebraic heritage.

---

3. Crossan, *Birth of Christianity*, xxi.

3. Recurring Questions

No study of Paul's letters leaves one free of questions. They remain inseparable from his legacy. A score might be cited, but the following questions ever recur.

(1) Just how much of his personal belief system did Paul "impose" on what he knew of the historical Jesus? "Impose" is not too strong a "charge" to level. Paul's own letters reveal that the direction he took was profoundly different from the views of Peter, James, and John. Only the latter's "in-God mysticism" would eventually prevail to soften Paul's stance on the end time and Christ as the promised Messiah and Fulfiller of God's will.

It was only with the ascendance of the gospels and the evangelists' attempts to portray Jesus as *a genuine flesh-and-blood Son of God* that Paul's more dogmatic vision of Jesus was contained and "replaced" by a more appealing human and personable Savior. Jesus' God-like presence, mystical forbearance, and forgiving nature replace the fervent rhetorical and authoritarian injunctions of Paul's system. The evangelists' Jesus speaks for himself, acts for himself, and attracts our allegiance by his sheer inimitable bearing. As such, he transcends the bounds of his own era and displays in his unique ontological *Dasein* the universal qualities that Paul so labored to apply. Truly he comes to us as God's gift, as a life that beckons us to love God and neighbor and not just the self, encouraging us to want to be like this person and possess his living presence as an ontological reality of our own. It is his life and love for all—the widowed, the lame, the blind, the lonely, and bereft, along with fishermen, mothers, carpenters, artisans, rabbis, and wealthy merchants—that steals into our souls and cleanses and heals them on his terms. No amount of propositional pleading can replace his compelling presence, nor can any emphasis on salvation, righteousness, faith, eternal life, or resurrection from the dead substitute for him and him alone. For that reason, Paul must always stand in his shadow and never supersede him, as great as Paul is. Yet the irony remains that without Paul, the gospels themselves might never have been written and may never have contained their

11. Fragments, Postulates, and Recurring Questions

long sections devoted to the passion narrative and Jesus' cross and resurrection. We owe that emphasis to Paul.

(2) An equally disturbing and irresoluble problem is why Paul rejected with such vehemence his nation's unique traditions and time-honored rituals that had defined Judaism for centuries. The numerous festivals, rites of thanksgiving, circumcision, and especially the revered tradition of Passover were designed to edify and renew his people's faith; they existed to remind them of God's ceaseless love and forbearance. Even Jesus refused to give up on the Law and its righteousness until God's kingdom should be fully established (Matt 5:17–20). Moreover, according to John's Gospel, there were at least three occasions we know of when Jesus celebrated the Passover in Jerusalem (John 2:13; 5:1; and 19:14). Did Paul find the casuistic Pharisaism of his day so misguided and misguiding, so self-righteous, heartless, and sterile, that he wanted nothing to do with its current form ever again and thus was willing to jettison his entire Hebraic heritage to reform it as no one could have imagined? In that sense, Paul's "reformation" was more irrevocable than Luther's. Yet having said that, according to Acts, he tirelessly visited synagogue after synagogue during his missionary journeys, and in his Letter to the Romans Paul longs for the day when Judaism will see the light. In essence, there is simply an enigmatic level to Paul that defies capture.

(3) Still, there remains an even larger unanswered question for contemporary Christianity. It concerns the value of any spiritual consciousness and ontological wholeness separated from Paul's "in-Christ mysticism." It is a question for all persons seeking deeper spiritual consciousness to ponder. Can the power of the Transcendent to transform human lives be effective without possessing an unassailable Ground of Being of its own? What is to redeem it from charges of mere idealism, or perspectivism? And if it has never disclosed or revealed itself in historical terms or in a historical event, then how does it attest to itself? How does it become the illuminating factor that ennobles existence and transforms lives?

Philosophically, the phenomenology of transcendence answers this question. Phenomenologically, we cannot help but put our existence to the question. We cannot help but examine the parameters of our existence and our being here, as Heidegger has so ably demonstrated and, for that matter, Marcel has shown in his awareness of our ontological search for an Order of the Spirit that makes sense of life.

For that reason, Paul's seven pillars of wisdom provide guidelines within which to accept the Transcendent's invitation to explore the heights and depths of existence. That is why his search for ontological wholeness, his openness to the sheer mystical and spiritual dimensions of existence, and his awareness of the Apollonian and Dionysian forces that either abet or thwart earthly dwelling continue to proffer universal norms for fulfillment. We *are* bound by time, and if there is anything eternal and good by which to live, only the arena of our present time provides the context in which that dream can be maximized.

That is why Paul is still worth reading, along with Plato, Aristotle, Augustine, Pascal, Heidegger, Marcel, Sartre, and Berdyaev. And yes, also Hawking, Edwards, von Hügel, Underhill, the Dalai Lama, and countless others. We are all part of the phenomenon of transcendence and the Transcendent's call to fulfill our lives.

Bibliography

Abernethy, George, and Thomas Langford. *Philosophy of Religion.* New York: Macmillan, 1962.
Aristotle. *Nicomachean Ethics.* Translated by Martin Ostwald. New York: Macmillan, 1962.
Armstrong, Karen. *A History of God.* New York: Ballantine, 1993.
———. *St. Paul: The Apostle We Love to Hate.* Icon Series. Boston: New Harvest, 2015.
Augustine. *Augustine: Confessions and Enchiridion.* Translated and edited by Albert Outler. Library of Christian Classics 7. Philadelphia: Westminster, 1955.
Barnstone, Willis, ed. *The Other Bible.* San Francisco: HarperSanFrancisco. 2005.
Berdyaev, Nicolas. *The Destiny of Man.* Translated by Natalie Duddington. New York: Scribner's Sons, 1937.
Bornkamm, Günther. *Paul.* Translated by D. W. G. Stalker. New York: Harper & Row, 1969.
Brenton, Lancelot C. L., ed. *The Septuagint with Apocrypha: Greek and English.* Grand Rapids: Zondervan, 1851.
Bruce, F. F. *Paul: Apostle of the Heart Set Free.* Grand Rapids: Eerdmans, 1977.
Burkert, Walter. *Greek Religion.* Translated by Natalie Duddington. New York: Scribner's Sons, 1937.
Cicero, Marcus Tullius. *On the Commonwealth.* In *Cicero's Tusculan Disputations,* translated by C. D. Yonge, 357–466. New York: Harper, 1877.
Crossan, John Dominic. *The Birth of Christianity.* New York: HarperSanFrancisco. 1998.
Gill, Richard, and Ernest Sherman, eds. *The Fabric of Existentialism: Philosophical and Literary Sources.* Englewood Cliffs, NJ: Prentice-Hall, 1973.
Gombis, Timothy G. *Paul: A Guide for the Perplexed.* London: T. & T. Clark, 2010.
Hamilton, Edith. *Mythology: Timeless Tales of Gods and Heroes.* New York: New American Library, 1942.
Harris, Stephen L. *The New Testament: A Student's Introduction.* 4th ed. Boston: McGraw-Hill, 2002.

Bibliography

Heidegger, Martin. *Existence and Being*. In *The Fabric of Existentialism: Philosophical and Literary Sources*, edited by Richard Gill and Ernest Sherman. Englewood Cliffs, NJ: Prentice-Hall, 1973.

———. *Poetry, Language, Thought*. Translated by Albert Hofstadter. New York: Perennial Classics, 1971.

James, William. *The Varieties of Religious Experience: A Study in Human Nature*. New York: Collier, 1961.

Kierkegaard, Søren. *Fear and Trembling; and The Sickness Unto Death*. Translated by Walter Lowrie. Garden City, NJ: Doubleday Anchor, 1954.

Kirwaczek, Paul. *Yiddish Civilisation: The Rise and Fall of a Forgotten Nation*. New York: Knof, 2005.

Lockhart, Ted. "W. D. Ross's Moral Theory." Lecture notes, n.d., Michigan Technological University. http://hu.mtu.edu/~tlockha/hu329ov8.

Marcel, Gabriel. *Being and Having*. In *The Fabric of Existentialism*, edited by Richard Gill and Ernest Sherman, 617–28. Englewoods, Cliffs, NJ: Prentice-Hall, 1973.

———. *Man Against Mass Society*. In *Existentialism*, edited by Robert Solomon, 124–33. New York: Modern Library, 1974.

Martin, Luther H. *Hellenistic Religions*. New York: Oxford University Press, 1987.

Mishima, Yukio. *The Decay of the Angel*. Translated by Edward G. Seidensticker. New York: Knopf, 1974.

Murphy-O'Connor, Jerome. *Paul: His Story*. London: Oxford University Press, 2005.

Nietzsche, Friedrich. *The Gay Science*. Translated by Walter Kaufmann. New York: Vintage, 1974.

Otto, Rudolf. *The Idea of the Holy*. Translated by John W. Harvey. New York: Galaxy, 1958.

Ross, William David. *The Right and the Good*. Oxford: Clarendon, 1930.

Sartre, Jean-Paul. *Being and Nothingness*. In *The Fabric of Existentialism*, edited by Richard Gill and Sherman, 492–508. Englewoods Cliffs, NJ: Prentice-Hall, 1973.

———. *Existentialism*. In *The Fabric of Existentialism: Philosophical and Literary Sources*, edited by Richard Gill and Ernest Sherman, 519–33. Englewood Cliffs, NJ: Prentice-Hall, 1973.

Schweitzer, Albert. *The Mysticism of Paul the Apostle*. Translated by William Montgomery. Baltimore: Johns Hopkins, 1998.

Seneca, Lucilius Annaei. *Moral Essays: In Three Volumes*. Translated by John W. Basore. Cambridge: Harvard, 1963.

Solomon, Robert, ed. *Existentialism*. New York: Modern Library, 1974.

Tillich, Paul. *Systematic Theology*. Vol. 1. Chicago: University of Chicago, 1951.

Underhill, Evelyn. *Mysticism: A Study in the Nature and Development of Spiritual Consciousness*. Mineola, NY: Dover, 2002.

Von Hügel, Friedrich. *The Mystical Element of Religion*. New York: Herder & Herder, 1999.

www.ingramcontent.com/pod-product-compliance
Lightning Source LLC
Chambersburg PA
CBHW050828160426
43192CB00010B/1938